T'AI CHI AS A PATH OF WISDOM

T'ai Chi

AS A PATH
OF WISDOM

Linda Myoki Lehrhaupt

SHAMBHALA
Boston & London
2001

SHAMBHALA PUBLICATIONS, INC.
Horticultural Hall
300 Massachusetts Avenue
Boston, Massachusetts 02115
www.shambhala.com

©2001 by Linda Myoki Lehrhaupt

9 8 7 6 5 4 3 2

Drawings of t'ai chi movements are used by permission of Loni Liebermann.
Drawings of the t'ai chi symbol are used by permission of Norbert Wehner.

Printed in the United States of America
♾ This edition is printed on acid-free paper that meets the
American National Standards Institute z39.48 Standard.
Distributed in the United States by Random House, Inc.,
and in Canada by Random House of Canada Ltd

Library of Congress Cataloging-in-Publication Data
Lehrhaupt, Linda Myoki.
T'ai chi as a path of wisdom / Linda Myoki Lehrhaupt.—1st ed.
p. cm.
Includes bibliographical references.
ISBN 1-57062-445-3 (pbk. : alk. paper)
1. T'ai chi. 2. Meditation. I. Title.
GV504 .L46 2001
613.7′148—dc21
2001020594

For Norbert and Taya

CONTENTS

ACKNOWLEDGMENTS

$\mathcal{A}$ philosopher recently advised me to keep this section short. Everyone knows that there are many people who have influenced anyone who writes a book. Perhaps. And yet I feel a strong urge to acknowledge my teachers and those people who have helped, influenced, and supported me. As I begin to write, I feel like I am an astronomer trying to name every light that twinkles in the evening sky. There have been many heavenly bodies in my universe, and so if you are of the same school of thought as my skeptical acquaintance, I invite you to move on and forego this opportunity to gaze at the stars.

Beginning at the beginning, I wish to thank the two people who crossed my path many years ago and whose love of t'ai chi gently touched me and started me on my own journey: first, to the man whose name I have forgotten but whose performance of the form at sunset on a mountaintop outside San Juan Bautista, California, in 1976 left me stunned and longing to know what he did. And to Tim Pitt, who introduced me to my first teachers and to a path with heart.

My first t'ai chi teachers, Ike and Pearl Coleman, manifested the body and soul of t'ai chi. They not only taught me the form and push hands, but they introduced me to the

precision and playfulness that can flow in this art. I feel
blessed to have been able to begin t'ai chi practice with such
gifted teachers.

I wish to extend my gratitude to Grand Master William
C. C. Chen, who taught me through his example what it
means to be a true man of the Tao. Not only was I fortunate
to benefit from his profound knowledge of t'ai chi in all its
aspects, but his example as a gifted, creative, and deeply kind
teacher left a lasting impression on me. I also wish to thank
him for the support he gave me all through the years as my
school developed in Germany, and for his teaching commitment to the ever larger number of students throughout Europe who train with him.

I feel a thankfulness beyond words to my chi kung
Teacher, Grandmaster B. P. Chan, for guiding me in the cultivation of this Taoist art. His vast knowledge of chi kung
was a continual source of nourishment to me. His painstaking
and exact teaching, flavored with his humor and deep sense
of caring for each student, touched me deeply. The spirit of
his dedication continues to flow through me. I hope it is in
a way that honors the legacy that he so generously shared
with us.

I owe a debt of gratitude to Dr. Tao Ping Siang, who came
three times to teach push hands in my school in Germany.
Dr. Tao's gentle and deeply sensitive approach to partner
training had a lasting impact on my ideas about push hands.
A special thanks goes to Andrew Heckert who assisted Dr.
Tao during these workshops and who later returned to teach
in my school.

Other t'ai chi and chi kung teachers with whom I have
been fortunate to train for very brief but fertile periods include Master Wang Yen-nien, Master Wei Lian, Dr. Shao

Xiadong, Dr. Josefine Zöller, Master Peter Ralston, and Master Cheung Chun Wa. Thank you also to Herve Marest, Sabine Metzle, and Ursula Meuser-Blauer, who taught me Master Wang's fan form. I also wish to thank my t'ai chi sisters and brothers who journeyed across the ocean to teach in my school and to allow us all to benefit from their many years of study with Master Chen: George Blank, Carol Mancuso, David Pancarician, and Laura Stone.

As the t'ai chi teacher training programs developed in my school, in addition to those teachers already mentioned, several others shared their expertise with trainees, enriching all of us in the process. I say thank you to Serge Dreyer, Linda Chase Broda, John Higginson, Epi van de Pol, Michael Plötz, Hans-Peter Sibler, and Stefan Suhr.

I am grateful to Maartje van Staalduijnen in Amsterdam and Luis Molera in Bremen, Germany, two senior European teachers of Master Chen's style, for their support and sharing over the years. The growth of Master Chen's style in Europe owes much to their dedication and commitment.

It would be impossible to thank all my students by name and so I will not try. But I want to acknowledge here that I have been graced by you in all your different manifestations: dedicated, lively, challenging, sometimes cantankerous, helpful, fun-loving and daunting. You have taught, cajoled, and humbled me down through the years. There were times when I leapt with joy and times when I wondered how I could ever go on. But you continued to flow like the dancing Bodhisattvahs that you are. With hands pressed together I bow to you in gratitude.

I was blessed in my beginning years of teaching to have a group of students who supported, challenged, and encouraged me to not only go deeper into my own t'ai chi and chi kung studies, but who were willing to make the same commitment to their training. I think of them fondly as the 6:00 A.M. group, because for several years we met every Wednesday morning to train intensively. Thank you to Tilman Baumstark, Axel Gripekoven, Barbara Hussong, Stefan Suhr, and Marlies Vollmer.

I also remember another series of early morning rendezvous in New York when I trained with Dennis Clark, my friend and fellow student of Master Chan, in a basement on the Lower East Side of Manhattan. Dennis graciously shared his knowledge as a senior student and taught me the secret of correction by his gentle and precise example.

To Jan Bosscher, my friend, training partner, and teacher in my school, I say thank you for all the years you have shared your friendship and knowledge, and especially for your support through the light and dark times.

To Karin Boskens another thank you for always keeping in touch and supporting me with good advice.

To my dear friend and colleague Sabine Stuckmann I say thank you from the bottom of my heart. Your generosity and support of my work has had a deep impact on my life. When I reached out to you for help you showed me how wide the arms of a Bodhisattvah can extend.

To Leslie Strickland, fellow countrywoman, t'ai chi and chi kung teacher and Dharma sister, I can only put my hands together and say Gassho for your generous spirit and understanding heart.

A debt of gratitude is owed to the sponsors of La Martinie, our retreat center in France; your support during the difficult years of getting started gave us the courage to go on.

To Marlies Vollmer, friend, colleague, Dharma sister and fellow traveler, I say thank you for being there for me and for being my friend. It has been a big support for me that we traveled down so many roads together.

To Mudita Wrede-Kapolke, who taught in the yearly t'ai chi groups in my school, I say thank you for your gentle and creative teaching, as well as those long phone conversations when you listened so patiently to me. To Karin Krudup, friend and colleague, I say thank you for your support and the exchange over so many years. And to the team women at BellZett in Bielefeld, Germany, I say it has been an honor to teach at such an innovative and dedicated institution for women.

To Geoff Pocock, my partner when I first began t'ai chi, I express my gratitude for your support and your commitment to do your very best for our daughter.

Many, many thanks to my editor at Shambhala Publications, Beth Frankl, for her careful reading of the manuscript and for her stimulating suggestions, which considerably improved the text. To my copyeditor, DeAnna Satre, I owe a great debt for helping me stay clear, concise, and on the right side of English grammar.

Several other persons read the manuscript in various stages and offered helpful comments. I wish to say thank you to Thomas Hallen, Loni Liebermann, Leslie Strickland, Mudita Wrede-Kapolke, and Sabine Stuckmann. I want to especially express my gratitude to Marianne Herzog and Helmi Düren, who made a heroic effort to read the exercises and descriptions and to suggest ways that they could be improved. I am, however, alone responsible for any lack of clarity that might occurr.

Loni Liebermann, the artist whose illustrations appear in this book, receives my heartfelt thanks for agreeing to allow her work to appear in this format. Her many years of experience as a t'ai chi and chi kung teacher, as well as her Zen practice, manifest in these pages.

There are no words to express my appreciation to my Zen teacher, Dennis Genpo Merzel, Roshi, Abbot of Kanzeon Sangha International. His example of commitment to transmitting the Dharma, his spirit of determination for all of his students to embody the teachings, and his efforts to explore the evolving forms Zen practice may take in modern America and Europe have been the deepest source of inspiration to me. Without his guidance, teaching, and example, I do not believe I could have written this book.

To my daughter, Taya, I wish to say thank you for your boundless support and encouragement. In times when I have faltered, you have prodded me to go on and not give up. Our relationship has taught me many things, and I am profoundly grateful that we have had the chance to learn together. Thank you for your clear-eyed wisdom and wide-open heart.

To my partner and husband Norbert I reserve these final words. I cannot begin to express what your love and commitment to our relationship over the past twenty years has meant to me. You are my anchor, though you always encourage me to fly. You have taught me the meaning of what it means to serve. Perhaps I learn the most from you as I watch you tend your plants and create oases of serenity. Thank you for teaching me how to water the garden.

INTRODUCTION

In this book I explore t'ai chi as a meditation practice and a path of wisdom and relate what we can learn about ourselves, others, and life itself when we study t'ai chi.

Almost everyone who practices t'ai chi for a period of time will tell you that what began as a weekly class in a movement exercise became a study in living and personal growth. T'ai chi is a path of wisdom meditation, but it is also a path with heart. As we walk this path we open our heart—to ourselves first and, then, like ripples spreading in a still pond, to everything and everyone around us. Tears sometimes mark the moments of great release and understanding and, ultimately, deep awakening. I believe that every moment of training is an opportunity to open, deepen, stretch, and grow. And at the core is a quiet voice that continually asks: "What is the heart of practice?"

When I began t'ai chi in 1978, it was the most difficult period of my life. Six months earlier I had given birth to my daughter, Taya, in a cesarean procedure with complications that left me exhausted for a long time afterward. Three months later my mother died, after living with breast cancer for eight years. Shortly afterward I left a secure and well-paying job to go on a three-month journey across America in a VW camping bus with my husband, Geoff, and Taya. Following the trip Geoff and I separated after twelve years of marriage. I settled down in a tiny apartment in New York, where my daughter slept in a windowed closet. I was twenty-nine years old, a single mother, and—along with my brother—the caretaker of a senile, elderly father. I didn't know it then but t'ai chi would touch every part of my life: it trained my body, opened my mind, and softened my heart. In fact, it saved my life.

In 1979 I began to study chi kung. What drew me to my first class was not the words *chi kung* on the announcement, because I had no idea what *chi kung* meant, but the word *meditation* written beneath. I was drawn to that first class as if the strongest force in the world were pulling me. From that point on, my chi kung and t'ai chi training intertwined. While people usually study either t'ai chi or chi kung, I have studied both almost from the beginning. For me the differences between the two are more about nuances and points of emphasis. Like the Buddhist metaphor of Indra's net, t'ai chi and chi kung are interrelated and yet each is unique.

Six months after starting chi kung, I attended my first introductory class in Zen meditation. My practice intensified over the years until, first, I received lay ordination, or jukai, in 1988, and then was ordained as a Zen priest in 1992. My sitting practice is the bedrock of my life and the ground from which many of the insights and perspectives in this book flow.

One of the reasons I initially began Zen practice was that I wanted to understand what the meditation in t'ai chi and chi kung was all about. As time wore on and my practice matured, I gave up trying to understand or figure things out and just continued my training. At the beginning I was searching; later my sitting practice prepared me to stop looking and just try to stay more open and receptive. From this well of not-knowing and not-planning, life happens. It is the same source that nourishes our t'ai chi once we learn to stop building dams and just let the river flow.

The only island of peace in my life in those early days was the time each day that I practiced t'ai chi. In those moments of quiet standing before beginning the sequence of movements that are the t'ai chi form something settled in me. My sense of struggle that came from caring for a young baby and an old man turned into a bright alertness. T'ai chi didn't make my problems go away, but it created a caring space in my life to which I could return each day to nourish my spirit and tend to my overworked body. T'ai chi gave me the tools to look at my life not as a desert but as a garden that I could cultivate; it gave me energy, patience, and a sense of timing.

In 1983 I moved to Germany, married again, and began to teach t'ai chi and chi kung. My students come from all walks of life and range in age from fifteen to seventy-nine. And while the reasons they begin training are very different, the reason they stay is always the same: through these arts they learn about themselves in a deep and challenging way. They come to appreciate their life as an opportunity to learn, grow, and flourish.

To appreciate our life means to be able to welcome both the storms and the gentle breezes of everyday life as part of living a life that matters. It means to explore deeply the idea of t'ai chi as a lifelong practice. Often beginning students misunderstand what this means. They think it refers to mastering the different t'ai chi forms or perfecting push hands technique. But as the stories in this book illustrate, t'ai chi has nothing to do with perfecting technique. It has nothing to do with mastering oneself, if by that we mean controlling our feelings or thoughts. It is, rather, the practice of the student who, frustrated and angry at not getting "it," starts to walk out the door but then returns to her training place and vows to try once more. Being able to say "I'll try again" is one of the deepest expressions of faith in oneself.

When we begin learning the t'ai chi form, one of the first things we come up against is our desire to learn quickly, effortlessly, and perfectly. As every beginning student soon finds out, however, it takes time, effort, and patience to learn t'ai chi. It asks us to dedicate a part of our day to ourselves, to practice even when we don't want to. It asks us to keep going, even when it looks like we're going nowhere. Most students who quit t'ai chi after studying for a short time do so not because t'ai chi is difficult to learn but because their expectations are not satisfied quickly enough. They leave because they do not want to face disappointment. Not wanting to feel the pain of disappointment is often what holds us back from trying our best. We are afraid to put our whole heart into something because we are afraid of breaking our heart. This is as true of studying t'ai chi as it is of anything in life.

In fact, learning t'ai chi is really a process of learning how to learn. This process is based on the understanding that what we discover about ourselves is just as important as simply performing a t'ai chi move correctly, if not more so. Learning how to learn includes developing the capacity to become intimate with our frustration and self-doubt. We see that what seemed like an obstacle can become an opportunity and, though small, can change our life entirely.

People often ask: "What are the benefits of learning t'ai chi?" When the student is a beginner, it is difficult to answer this question in a deep way. In fact, most prospective students usually know what they want: stress reduction, physical exercise, correction of alignment or posture problems, a form of self-defense, instruction in a Taoist art; these are among the most common reasons. But the hidden treasure of t'ai chi is not something that many students are seeking to begin with. To find this treasure asks nothing short of commitment, engagement, discipline, and a willingness to keep going, even when the goal seems far away and obscured. However, as students train, they learn that each class offers an opportunity to search in a very practical way for all the parts of themselves that are blocked, to look at their preconceptions and face their reactions in a new way. That is at the heart of what it means to practice t'ai chi.

This book is organized into seven parts, which are named after classical movements that appear in almost every style of t'ai chi. The chapters in each part were inspired by and reflect themes appropriate to that particular movement, or to t'ai chi practice in general. The chapters may include a story about a teacher or student or concerning a point about the movement itself, or a reflection or association from my own life and work as a t'ai chi teacher. In an effort to protect their privacy, I have changed the names of most people and created some composite figures. All of the situations described are true, though a few have been embellished in order to make a point.

The chapters—some of which are lightly pondering, while others are more fiery—are meant to be commentaries that one can return to again and again. In that sense they share some of the qualities of the t'ai chi classical texts, which are read repeatedly, each time revealing something new as one's skill advances or understanding deepens. I conclude each part with an exercise or exercises that allow the reader to experience the theme I have just developed. These exercises can be a resource both for students and for teachers who may be looking for additional means to teach the basic themes of t'ai chi. However, one does not have to know t'ai chi to do the exercises; they are also useful for teachers and students in other movement or martial arts.

At the beginning of each of the seven parts, I include a description of a t'ai chi movement from the form that I have practiced since 1978. This form is taught by my teacher, Grand Master William C. C. Chen, one of America's most experienced and dedicated teachers. Grand Master Chen was a student of Professor Cheng Man-ch'ing, with whom he began his training in Taiwan when he was a teenager. For those of you who wish to see photographs of the form, please consult Master Chen's book *Body Mechanics of T'ai Chi Chuan*. The illustrations of t'ai chi movements at the beginning of each part are not always identical to the movements described. In any case, they are meant to transmit the spirit and quality of the t'ai chi movements rather than be precise representations.

The appendix includes answers to some of the most frequently asked questions about how to practice t'ai chi. It also includes suggestions for how to establish a regular practice rhythm and how to face the most common events or situations that tend to sidetrack and sometimes derail our practice.

Although I use t'ai chi as a reference point in this book, it is possible to transpose the things I say about it to almost anything that is learned or practiced with mindfulness. This includes chi kung, aikido, karate, yoga, dance, learning to play a musical instrument, knitting, cooking, mowing the lawn, or painting a house. It is not the act that makes something a meditative practice but the way and the state of mind with which it is executed. Thus the list of relevant activities is endless, and so are the possibilities in life to learn and grow.

One of the central points of t'ai chi as a path of wisdom is finding our way to being at home with who we are. In the beginning we often approach learning t'ai chi with a self-critical attitude that does not allow us to be either patient or comfortable with ourselves. We apply the competitive spirit that is so valued in our world, leading us to judge ourselves constantly, to set up standards of discipline that are difficult to attain, or to undermine ourselves with harsh critical comments. But as Pema Chödrön, a Tibetan Buddhist teacher, writes so beautifully in *The Wisdom of No Escape*, "Meditation practice isn't about trying to throw ourselves away and become something better. It's about befriending who we are already."[1]

If we practice t'ai chi as a path of wisdom, we will see that it continually asks us to open to ourselves and to let go of those destructive ideas and acts that weaken our spirit and undermine our intention. It will lead us through a process of acknowledging our strengths without pride and recognizing our weaknesses without scorn. To work with ourselves in this way feels exactly the same as when we help a baby stand up after she has fallen down. We take her by the hand and wait patiently for her to stabilize on her own two feet. Then we give her a big kiss, let go of her hands, and say, "Go ahead, sweetie. Try again!" That is the heart of practice.

INVITATION

Imagine that you have invited a friend to dinner. She's an ally from the old days, someone you have shared most of life's ups and downs with. When she arrives she seems to be very tired. Up all night with the baby, she has spent most of the day cramming for an exam. Her back hurts and her head is full of thoughts about an upcoming job interview. She can't stay too long, she apologizes, because she has to get up early for work.

After dinner you take a walk together along the East River, going as far as the Brooklyn Bridge. It's a starry summer night. The park along the river is full of New Yorkers enjoying the breeze from the river. The air is filled with the hum of the city. As the lights beckon across the river in Brooklyn, you both enjoy these most wonderful moments of living in the Big Apple.

Without speaking you take your positions to start the form. After all, you are t'ai chi sisters, having trained for many years with the same master. You stand for some moments taking it all in: the stars, the tugboats, the cars on the bridge, babies, promotions, traffic. As you do the form, the universe is dancing the moment with you. The moon rises above the horizon just as you finish. Without knowing why, you bow. From that moment on, you know that you will always end the form with a bow.

Now imagine that the special friend you invited to do t'ai chi is yourself. If we can think of our t'ai chi practice as an invitation to someone dear to us, it will help us to take care of ourselves as we would a good friend. If a friend is tired or hungry, we help him or give her something to eat. If he feels low, we try to be there for him. If her muscles are tight, we get out the body oil and clear the dining table to serve as a massage table. It all happens, it all unfolds, because we naturally want to support a friend.

When you stand up to do the form you are being there for yourself as you would be there for a friend if she or he needed you. It is extremely helpful to think in these terms because it encourages us to be kind to ourselves. It helps to counter a tendency to want to run away from practicing because we are afraid of failing or because it's too lonely to train by ourselves. When we treat our t'ai chi practice as an opportunity to dance all aspects of our life, we embrace it all, just as we embraced the magic of the night under the Brooklyn Bridge.

Preparation

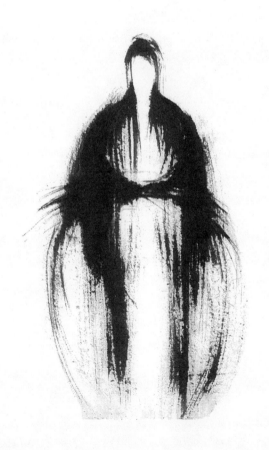

*P*reparation appears to be a relatively simple move, but it is difficult to execute well. It is difficult not because the move is tricky, but because it asks us to be completely present, attuned to ourselves and the environment around us. It invites us to sink our roots into the moment. It encourages us not to rush to start, which is often a rush to finish. It is a body mantra, which supports us in being "right here, right now!"

When you learn the first movement of a form, which usually involves standing quietly before beginning to move, some mention will be made of the t'ai chi posture. It can often sound like a kind of drill as your teacher says things like, "Stand as if you are suspended from above by a golden thread attached to the top of your head. The shoulders are relaxed, your ears are in line with your shoulders, nose over the navel, your chin drawn ever so slightly in. The breast bone is slightly raised and gently pushing forward, the lower back is long, and the buttocks are tucked under. Your feet are firmly planted on the floor and the toes are relaxed. Your eyes are looking straight ahead in a soft gaze."

In taking the t'ai chi posture it is wise to remember that we are not machines, clothing dummies, or statues. We can never fix a posture or indeed the form so that is set forever, but we can explore it continually. The posture as a whole in t'ai chi will be a constant teacher throughout our practice: it will please us, satisfy us, frustrate, charm, and defeat us, all at once or one at a time and every variation in between. There is no one point where you can freeze it or say that it will never change. We may want to have that kind of security, but knowing that it doesn't exist is also a kind of freedom. When we really accept this, we are accepting one of t'ai chi's gifts to us.

So take your time as you assume the beginning stance of Preparation. You've got a whole t'ai chi life ahead of you.

Begin Preparation by standing with your heels touching so that your feet form a V shape and your arms are hanging at your sides, the palms facing the body. There is space under the arms, as much as if you would place your own closed fist to rest there. The third finger of each hand is in line with the middle of your outer thigh. The hands have a delicate shaping to them, as if each one were holding a rice dish. This hand posture allows for space between the fingers as well as a sense of a soft stretch in the palms. Master William C. C. Chen likes to describe the hands in t'ai chi as "dancing palms," which communicates a sense of the light energy that enlivens and activates the form.

Now drop your weight into the right leg. Rather than shifting the weight, which often involves moving the hips too much, think more about letting the weight sink. Imagine that you are standing on a wet beach, and without moving you want to create a deep impression with your right foot.

Then take a step with the left foot and place it pointing straight ahead and a shoulder's width from the right foot. The weight is still mostly on the right leg. Then ease almost all your weight onto the left foot. Then turn on the heel of the right foot so that the toes point forward, and your right foot is parallel to the left foot. At the same time, turn both hands so that they point backward. Keep the space under the arms.

The fingers continue to have a slight roundness. The weight is in the middle of both feet.

The position when we are standing with our feet parallel and the palms are facing the body is called the Wu Chi stance. This is one of the most familiar standing meditation postures. *Wu Chi* refers to the Taoist idea of the origin of the universe, and is the name given to the moments of endless time before all the elements took form. *Wu Chi* can also be translated as the Mother of All Possibilities. It is a moment of immense potential, waiting and extending throughout all space and time.

The Wu Chi stance embodies an attitude that is the foundation of our practice: It is one of attention to the moment, a listening inward and a listening outward at the same time. We are resting in stillness and silence and yet ready to be fully in the movement that is to come.

1
Waiting at the Entrance

Entrances, or gates, are often fraught with difficulty. They can take many forms: the birth canal, the decompression chamber of a rocket ship, a hole in the ice made by Eskimos to return the animal spirits to their ancestors. They can lead to initiation huts, gambling halls, and bedrooms of bliss. The time when we are in the entrance area or going through the door is a time of being between worlds. Victor Turner, a great anthropologist of modern times, would have called it being "betwixt and between." We have not completely left one state, nor are we at home in the new one.

Waiting at the entrance is a time of expectancy. We wait to get married, to enter an oral examination, to get a ticket for a hot concert, to hear the last long breath before someone dies. When we enter through a gate, we can never know for sure what we will find inside. That is why, in all cultures, entrances are considered dangerous places. Rituals have been developed throughout human life to safeguard the passage through them.

But as varied as these rituals are, they all share the goal of supporting a person to go through the gate. They are not created to prevent someone from doing so, nor are they meant to take away the difficulties. Those who created the rituals knew that to make things easier would rob the entrant of the initiatory power of the transition. That power lies in the faith and sense of accomplishment that is generated when one has "arrived." It's the same feeling whether one has run a marathon, fixed an engine that wouldn't start, won the presidential election, or taken one's first step as a baby. It's just a question of degree.

When you begin to practice t'ai chi, you have entered through a gate. As the weeks and months go by, things may go smoothly. One feels that progress is being made, especially as one gets closer to the end of the form. And then suddenly there is another entrance, or gate. It's often at the point where a move you may have practiced twenty times still feels awkward or you've forgotten how it goes or you've skipped it completely.

Suddenly what felt like a great undertaking now feels like a big mess. You just want to chuck the whole thing! Now the gate is an exit to an easier life, a life where you don't torture yourself trying to learn some stupid Chinese movement art. The only movement meditation you want to practice is raising and lowering a glass of wine as you sit in a French café and watch the farmer's market being disbanded on a glorious Thursday summer afternoon.

At this moment we are standing in front of a door marked "Impatience, Illusion, Frustration." Can we continue to wait at the entrance, without either rushing through the door or running back where we came from? Can we accept the invitation to learn about ourselves that waiting offers us, including taking everything that happens as part of the situation, rather than accepting some things and rejecting others? Can we not rush to get to the end of waiting but take it moment by moment?

John Tarrant writes eloquently in his book *The Light Inside the Dark* of the power of waiting:

> When we are blocked, when circumstances are not ripe, we have to find some way of acknowledging that we are waiting, that we are pregnant and not merely asleep. Pausing like this is at the heart of meditation practice. When we attend closely to our lives, though it seems that nothing is happening, in the subterranean currents, reconciliation is setting off, invisible until the moment of its arrival. This waiting is not an effort at working a problem through, nor is it getting out of the way—it is being in the way just a little, just enough to allow the universe to work the problem through.[1]

We can dilute the power of waiting when we try to shorten it, prolong it, or change it to another day. When we are truly ready to just wait at the entrance, we learn that waiting itself is the entrance. Then, when the door opens, we go in and sit down. When the meeting is over, we get up and leave. Beginning and ending the t'ai chi form is no different. It only looks that way.

2

Preparing to Pay Attention

It's natural to think that Preparation, the first movement, is about preparing to begin the t'ai chi form. But I like to think it's about preparing to pay attention.

We prepare by centering and settling, allowing the flurry of everyday thoughts and our body's rhythms to find a quieter, deeper level. We can use the standing position at the beginning of the movement Preparation as a mindfulness exercise to scan our body carefully and be aware of the sensations in each part. Beginning with the feet and working upward to the crown of our head in a step-by-step process, we train a faculty for careful attention that we can apply later when doing our form. Being aware of the moment-to-moment changes in feeling, concentration, and muscle tension helps us to be aware not only of ourselves but also of the miraculous complexity of each particle of life.

Standing meditation, of which there are several types, generally helps to calm our thoughts. We may stand as long as we feel comfortable, but one to two minutes at the beginning of Preparation is a good general rule of thumb. One image I use to describe what happens during the standing meditation is to compare it to sand dropping to the bottom of a glass of water. The sand settles, particle after particle, some being heavier than others. Eventually all the sand lies at the bottom. It will stay there if we do not stir it up too much. It's the same with our busy thoughts. They too settle as we continue to stand.

Traditionally the t'ai chi classics, a series of texts written by masters down through the centuries, tell us that in the standing posture we should imagine that we are hanging from above by a golden string attached to the crown of our head. This image is meant to help us sense that our body is light and in natural alignment. If we think of the spine as a string of pearls being held from above, then each vertebra, like the pearls, is in alignment but not pressing down on the next.

It takes time, though, to feel the alignment in the standing posture in a naturally relaxed way. Some students feel uncomfortable in the beginning. The legs may tremble; there may be stiffness in the shoulders, feet, or calves. Most of the time these problems ease with practice, though they can reappear again or others can predominate.

There's an important lesson to be learned in the early stages of standing meditation. It is an opportunity to face and to learn to work with uncomfortable sensations, boredom, or even pain. Normally we want to get rid of these unpleasant sensations or change them into pleasant ones. This thought alone creates a great deal of restlessness; it does not allow us to settle into the posture. When, however, we pay careful attention to our sensations, study them, even awaken a curiosity about them, we see that they are very different from the solid wall of pain or discomfort that we imagined. They increase, decrease, sharpen, are relieved, or change location. We are in touch with the moment-to-moment process of change, shifting, and movement. This in turns help to loosen the fear that we will be trapped in pain forever. It helps us to see that a situation can be difficult but it can also flow.

An experience from my own life may help ground what I have to say in everyday terms.

In 1988 I was experiencing one of the most stressful periods of my life. I was juggling a career, raising a child, trying to finish a doctoral dissertation, and supporting our family as my husband studied full-time. I was in deep conflict about whether to complete the dissertation. My conflict stemmed from the fact that I had decided not to work in the field of my academic training but instead to develop a teaching career in t'ai chi and chi kung.

At the time of my story I had gone to stay in the guest house of a Franciscan monastery in southern Germany so I could work on my dissertation. It took a few days for me to calm down, but finally I felt settled enough to begin writing. But it did not go well. I was still unclear about why on earth I was finishing the dissertation.

The pressure continued to build in the month that I stayed there. One morning around 1:00 A.M. as I was working I began to hear a strange noise, a high-pitched whistle. I searched the room to find its source but could not find anything. After a while the noise stopped.

Suddenly around 3:00 A.M. I heard it again. I realized that the sound was not in the room but inside my head. I spent most of the night practicing every mental and relaxation technique I could think of, but the whistle did not go away; rather, it increased in volume.

The noise level in my ears got worse as the months went by. The doctor diagnosed tinnitus, known commonly as ear ringing. "You'll just have to learn to live with it," she said. But I refused. I spent every moment of every day for months trying to shut out the noises. The noises and my stressed efforts to silence them took over my life.

During a sesshin (an intensive silent retreat) later that year, I poured out the whole story to my Zen teacher. When I finished, he guided me through a meditation in which I gradually turned my complete attention to my hearing. "Just listen," he said. "Don't shut out the sounds. Just let them come."

I was able to go ahead and experience the thing I feared the most. The sounds got louder until my head filled with them. But unlike the other times, I was able to listen to them without the gripping fear I normally felt. When I wasn't fighting them, the sounds were not the threatening mass of noise I had thought they were. At the end of the meditation they were still present but not so disturbing as they had been.

I learned a lesson that day that has stayed with me down through the years. Now, more than a decade later, my tinnitus is not gone, but it has found a place in my life. When I am tired or have been pushing myself too much, the sounds get louder and work their way into my attention. They alert me to the need to take care of myself. So instead of fighting off the sounds, I listen to them. And I listen to myself.

In the same way, the difficulties that might occur during the standing meditation are an opportunity to observe, open to, and be present for whatever comes up. As we learn not to push them away, we notice that they are constantly changing, shifting, expanding. Just the insight that small shifts are constantly taking place shows us that ease or disease are not fixed but are in a constant movement between these polarities.

Such an experience can not only train us to do standing meditation but also teach us the most skillful approach to working with more difficult emotions, such as fear. When we really feel fear and let it be present, it loosens its grip, which is caused by the tension of our obsessing, worrying, or trying to control it. It no longer feels like a huge mass that is oppressing us. It feels more open, spacious, and fluid, which has a relaxing quality in itself.

I don't want to give the impression that opening to fear, illness, or pain is easily accomplished, especially when we are facing something as serious as chronic pain, life-threatening illness, or psychological trauma. Sometimes we may need psychotherapy or other forms of guidance, and it is important to seek them out when necessary. But while it is not easy to open to fear or pain, that doesn't mean that we should not start. I simply want to encourage you to explore every dimension of t'ai chi practice as an opportunity to pay attention—to experience life and yourself in all their fullness.

3

The Quiet before Dawn

The moments just before sunrise are magical. A faint glow appears in the eastern sky. The light increases slowly but steadily as the world hovers between night and day. There is a stillness that stretches to infinity. Nothing is lacking in the moments before dawn.

Watching the sunrise is considered a sacred act in many religious traditions. Pilgrimages to holy sites are often timed to include a high point when the community of pilgrims watch the sunrise together. The climbing of Mount Fuji in Japan is a well-known example, with pilgrims beginning their ascent at night so as to reach the summit by dawn. I once saw a photo of a Mount Fuji pilgrim bowing to the sun at the moment it appeared on the horizon. His bow was a gracious act of welcome, acknowledging that he and the sun were not two. Bowing to the sun, he bowed to himself.

As part of my doctoral research on pilgrimage, I climbed to the summit of Croagh Patrick on the west coast of Ireland three times. Although Catholic pilgrims climb the mountain throughout the year, the main day of pilgrimage is always the last Sunday in July, when anywhere from forty thousand to eighty thousand people climb in one day. By the time of my research in the mid-1980s, the pilgrimage no longer began at midnight as it had for centuries. The church hierarchy had intervened to end the nocturnal pilgrimage, mainly out of concern for safety. In my interviews with elderly pilgrims, almost all mentioned that this was the thing they missed the most. They especially mourned the lost spirit of camaraderie fostered by the journey up the mountain in darkness, with only candles or kerosene lamps to light the way.

Watching the sunrise from the top of Croagh Patrick at dawn was spectacular. One pilgrim told me:

> It was not the sun coming up that moved me so much, although that was beautiful. It was those moments before, when the world was so still. Looking out from the summit I saw the whole of Westport Bay alive with life, the birds flying majestically, yet because we were on the summit, we didn't hear them. There was a natural quiet, as if all the life on earth were engaging in a silent tribute to the day that was to begin. Those still moments before dawn were full with the promise of activity that was to come. I have never known another such magical moment.

The moments we stand quietly before beginning the t'ai chi form are as full as those moments before dawn on Croagh Patrick. There is stillness but also a sense of movement within. In the standing posture we can sense what the ancient Taoists knew intuitively: that a human being is a channel that connects heaven and earth. According to Taoist philosophy, the heaven energy of yang and the earth energy of yin flow into the body through the head and feet respectively and meet in the tan tien, the energy center located near the navel. The dance and merging of energies that take place are symbolized by the yin-yang symbol.

This quiet standing at the beginning of the form is a time of centering and grounding. The tensions of the day that lodge in our body flow downward and into the ground. At the same time, the earth is supporting us to stand tall like a tree, with our branches reaching to touch the sky. It is helpful to stand with the image of a tree in our mind's eye and to feel the lengthening of the body, but we must be careful not to force it.

Normally we think preparation means getting ready to do something. But if we go to the heart of what Preparation really is, we see that it is exactly the opposite. We prepare by doing nothing. In t'ai chi we prepare to move by first deepening into stillness.

It doesn't matter where you are at the moment when you stand in Preparation to begin the form. You may be on the summit of a great mountain or on a grass patch in a city park. Wherever you are, be alive to the vibrancy of the moment. When you do begin, the movements will extend endlessly, as a Buddhist sutra says, beyond all space and time.

4

Standing on Your Own Two Feet

The t'ai chi form has much to teach us about balance—and about standing on our own two feet. Almost every movement has us shifting our weight from one leg to another, from heel to toe or vice versa. Ideally, no matter where we are when moving, our body is in alignment and we feel rooted through the feet. In reality many of us have to learn again what it means to stand in a stable and centered way, the way we stood as babies, with our center low to the ground. Thus when a beginners class experiments with shifting their weight, many a student at first moves so that his knee extends way over whichever foot is forward. When he shifts his weight onto the back leg, his rear end often hangs over the heel of the back foot. In either position there is no real stability.

To help students find their point of balance, I have them do an exercise where they begin shifting their weight forward and backward. First they move to the extreme of each position. As they shift through the middle, I ask them to notice the point where they feel most balanced, then to move beyond it. The forward and backward movements become smaller until the person finds herself settling into her middle.

Finding the point where the body stands in natural balance and alignment is an important discovery in t'ai chi. It has implications not only for the moment but for our entire life.

One of the greatest teachings I had on this subject was when I worked with a woman who had polio as a young child. Her right arm was limp and she could not put weight on her right foot. She wanted to learn t'ai chi because she found the movements beautiful. "I know I won't be able to do it like the others," she said, "but I would like to try."

She spent two years learning the form. We devised ways whereby she could execute the movements by making some adjustments to the form. Working slowly, aided by the increased balance and coordination she developed over months of training, she succeeded in putting some weight on her right foot.

At the end of two years, she said that the most important thing she had learned was that she was not as physically handicapped as she thought she was. This understanding caused her to reassess her whole life. She decided to get her driver's license, then haggled with a health-insurance company until it agreed to pay the cost of equipping a car she could drive. Then she quit her job and found a new one that was more challenging, both physically and mentally. Eventually she stopped t'ai chi because she was now so busy that her free time was limited. She went on to study African dancing!

The improved balance that results from studying t'ai chi has ramifications in many areas of life. One important study in this respect was a research project I heard about in which elders learned t'ai chi. One of the findings was that the number of falls was significantly reduced in the t'ai chi group as compared with the control group. For elders, incapacitation as a result of falling is one of the most threatening events of mature life and one that often leads to the loss of independence and/or the capacity to live in one's own home.

I remember vividly another student who began t'ai chi because he wanted to improve his balance. He was in his early thirties and had been born without arms. Small hands protruded from each shoulder, the sadly familiar result of his mother having taken thalidomide when she was pregnant.

I met Bob early in my teaching career and so the whole situation was very new to me. I couldn't understand why he wanted to learn t'ai chi. The arms play such an important role in expressing the movements. How would he enjoy doing the form?

Bob taught me a very important lesson about not dwelling on limitations. From the first class, he was the most enthusiastic, most resilient student and the one who practiced the most. Through working with him, I came to see how much we rely on the arms for balance. Because he had no arms, his center of balance had to be low in his belly. Indeed, he epitomized the t'ai chi maxim of moving from the *tan tien*.

Though his sense of balance was excellent, he tended to hold himself rigidly in the lower body area around the hips and waist. As I encouraged him to turn more from the lower body, which freed up his hips and waist, he lost some of his balance capabilities for a short time. It was actually a natural readjustment process that comes when we change a habitual movement pattern. He approached the new challenge with enthusiasm and experimented freely. Sometimes his balance was so shaky, I was afraid he would fall over. Several times I had to resist running to steady him as he swayed precariously during a move.

By the end of the first year, he had much greater movement in his lower body. As a result of feeling more secure when moving, he felt encouraged to take up other sports, including skiing, that he had avoided in the past. He now felt more confident that he could handle the challenge.

It's an illusion to think this sense of having limited capability is confined to people with special needs. It may be more acute, but it is not unique to this population. I have known so many students who emphasize what they can't do. In many cases they have been taught this from the earliest days of their childhood. Lack of self-esteem is the name that currently sums up this psychological epidemic in our society. In emphasizing all the reasons why we can't do t'ai chi, we are taking the same attitude as a person who always notices that the glass is half empty rather than rejoicing that it is half full.

We would all do well to internalize the outlook emphasized at the Stress Reduction Clinic of the University of Massachusetts Memorial Medical Center in Worcester, Massachusetts, where patients are encouraged to think from the very beginning: "There's more right with me than wrong with me." They are not being asked to deny the serious medical or psychological conditions that have brought them to the clinic; the phrase is simply meant to help them be clear about one fact: In the totality of their lives, illness is only one part. Without this continuous reminder, an illness can take over our life, until it determines who we are and what we can do. The way others treat us, both in the medical environment and at home, may accentuate our view of ourselves as limited. But that doesn't make it true.

I don't know how many versions I've heard of the basic refrain: "I can't learn this because I am too . . ." (fill in the blank). But we are not clumsy, stupid, out of balance, stubborn, incapable, untalented, or a klutz from day one. That is not our basic nature, though this attitude toward ourselves may have been with us for so long that it feels that way. While there are so many lessons that t'ai chi can teach us, rediscovering our true balance is one of its most precious gifts. A balanced posture embodies and manifests our natural sense of dignity. We no longer need to hold, tighten, or defend ourselves against the pull of gravity. We experience a sense of natural grace, which is our birthright. Like the tree sending its branches to the sky, like the bird who rides on the wind, we are centered and yet extending in all directions. When we experience this even for a moment, it will inspire us for the rest of our lives.

5

Not Pretty, Just Chi

We were sitting in Madison Square Garden, surrounded by thousands of would-be Bruce Lees. Some of the younger men in the audience were wearing kung fu clothing, with nunchakus (one-foot-long wooden sticks originally hinged with silk cords, now generally hinged with a chain) hanging precariously out of their back pockets. On the street they could be stopped, even arrested, for carrying such a deadly weapon. But we didn't need to worry about them causing any trouble in the Garden—the center was full of martial arts teachers. Any of them would have reveled at having one just cause to lay a troublemaker flat out.

A group of us went to watch a performance by a wu shu (martial arts) troupe from China. The two-hour extravaganza we were about to view would be one of the first times that a Western audience would get to see in the flesh what they normally saw only in the movies. Chinese movies. The kind that played continuously to packed houses in the theaters of Chinatown.

I was excited to be in the Garden and to be able to see the future stars of the kung fu movies in real life. The perform- ance began with the youngest members, some as young as seven, doing the impossible. As the show went on, the age of the performers increased gradually, and so did the complexity of their routines. We watched dazzling displays of skill that could only be called miraculous. If I hadn't seen it with my own eyes, I would have said that it was impossible. And yet it all looked so easy.

I sat next to a t'ai chi and chi kung teacher from China. A friend of mine had studied with him there and then invited him to New York for an extended visit. I turned to look at his face. He seemed to be enjoying the show. He especially liked the young kids. From time to time he would point to one of them, smile broadly, and say, "Good! Good!"

During the break we continued to sit while others went to get drinks and something to eat. I took the opportunity to ask my friend's teacher what he thought of the wu shu troupe.

"Very pretty, but not chi," he said immediately. He caught the look of surprise in my eyes and went on to explain.

"Their attention is only on the outside. To look good. They train and train to make the outside look pretty. But look how they stand. No roots! Look how they move: fast but empty."

I was stunned by his words. I had spent the last hour mesmerized by their feats. How could it be possible to do all that and not have chi (life energy, or vital force)? How could they do all those complicated jumps and partner routines and not be rooted? They seemed as if their feet were bolted to the floor. At least it looked that way to me. I decided to get further clarification.

"I don't understand. Surely they have chi. Otherwise how could they do all these things?"

"Yes, they have pretty chi. But it is not true chi. It is like those young boys and girls who fly through the air [he was

referring to a gymnastics competition we had watched together on TV]. Very beautiful. But not chi. Just pretty chi."

I remained puzzled throughout the rest of the second half.
Older martial artists, perhaps in their early twenties, continued to amaze us. But after about fifty minutes, the whole
show came to an abrupt halt. Three men moved a large stone
into place near center stage. A chair and a huge sledgehammer were also placed near the boulder, which was lifted
onto a trestle.

"Ladies and gentlemen," began the announcer, "to end our
show, we are going to be honored with a special demonstra-
tion of chi kung, China's ancient system of internal mastery
and the mother of all the martial arts. We ask you to be quiet
and not move about unnecessarily. The master requires a still
and concentrated atmosphere to perform his incredible feat."

After a few moments a rather short, stocky Chinese man
appeared onstage. He was dressed in plain pants and a
T-shirt. An assistant came running from behind and tried to
hand him a black cotton jacket, similar to what most Chinese
martial artists wear, but he waved him away. Something
about the whole scene was strange. I kept looking at the master, wondering what was so different. Then I realized in a
flash—his hair was gray. In all these two hours, I had not
seen on the stage one person old enough to have gray hair.

I turned to look at my friend's teacher. He was alert and
sitting upright on the edge of his seat. He scrutinized the
stage with an eagle-eye attentiveness. It was the first time during the whole evening that he had appeared like the gentle but
fiercely exact warrior that I knew him to be. Fierce, not because he tried to dominate his students, but because he used
his energy to help them to be the very best they could be.

My eyes turned back to the stage. The younger man

picked up the sledgehammer. He approached the granite stone, raised the mallet high, and letting out a startling cry, hit the stone with tremendous power. The rebound from his slam threw him across the stage. The stone, which he was apparently meant to split in two, was doing just fine.

The master pulled a stool in front of the stone and sat down. He laid his forehead against the stone. He continued to sit with his eyes closed for several moments. He laid his hands on his navel. Without being reminded again, the audience quieted down to the point where you could hear a chopstick drop.

It was over before it began. A slight movement of his head, quicker than a jackhammer, and the stone split in two, falling with a crash onto the stage. Thousands of people gasped as one! Then a stunned silence. Slowly the cheers swelled, eventually filling the hall. The audience jumped to its feet, clapping wildly. Many shouted Bravo! Bravo!

The master simply stood at the center of the stage, his head bowed, receiving the ovation. Then he slowly walked off, turning for a moment and bowing deep to the crowd before disappearing behind the curtain.

I looked at my neighbor, who did not clap but stood at rapt attention, his eyes fixed squarely on the master until he left. As the crowd quieted and we waited to exit our row, he turned to me and said: "Now you see the difference!" I waited, hoping he would explain more of what was obvious to him but still miserably eluding me.

He seemed to understand and took compassion on me. "I said before, the others have no chi. They just look pretty. But now you see the difference. He is just the opposite: not pretty, just chi!"

From that night on, the words "just pretty, no chi" became

a standard part of this teacher's assessment of his students' skill. I had been joining his early morning classes in the park as a guest, so I also heard these words time and time again. My whole training became focused on doing whatever was necessary to avoid hearing them, or at least to avoid their being applied to me.

I took to practicing in front of a mirror, determined to do the movements perfectly. The summer vacation had just begun. I was obsessed with the idea that by the first of September the words "just pretty, no chi" would never cross his lips again in reference to me. I became fanatical about millimeter exactness, doing moves over and over again if there seemed to be even the slightest rough edge to them. I felt like a moving sculpture that I could chip away at to make its contours perfect.

I applied the same kind of determination to my standing meditation. My friend's teacher had drummed into us that it was the most important exercise we could do. I stood in front of the mirror at the beginning of each training period. I even made lines on the glass so that I could match my arms to the exact height and angle each time. My daughter, who was just two at the time, would sometimes wander in and stand in front of me, mimicking my movements. It was a treat to see a toddler in diapers and T-shirt raising her small arms and standing like Kung Fu Baby.

In those days we met once a week in the park for early morning practice. Usually Taya was in nursery school, but on one particular morning the school was closed. I took her with me to class and hoped to keep her busy with toys and other playground distractions while we practiced.

We began, as usual, with standing meditation. As we all stood in lines so that the teacher could adjust our posture,

Taya took her position in front of me and raised her arms in the standing position. She was at the point where she could hold it for a minute, which was really quite a feat for a normally squirming, joyfully busy toddler.

As the teacher approached, I could hear him chuckling with delight. He came quickly toward us and focused all his attention on her. "You see," he said to me, "you follow the baby. She knows the secret."

"What secret?" I asked, through slightly clenched teeth. We had already been standing for quite some time.

"You remember that master who chopped the stone in two with his head? He had it. And she has it."

"What do they have?" I asked, rather frustrated.

"Chi! Look how she stands! She's perfect. Like sitting on a stool. Feet with roots in the earth." Taya began waddling away, a bit bored with all this meaningless conversation.

"Look at the way she walks!" the teacher said excitedly. "Full of chi."

I happened to know that she was walking like that because her diaper was full of something else besides chi. The weight of it all was probably causing her to sink down more than anything else. At least, that's what I wanted to believe.

The next day in the privacy of my home I changed my whole way of practicing standing meditation. I no longer stood in front of the mirror. Rather than pay attention to the outward shape of my posture, I focused on what it felt like on the inside. I tried various visualization techniques— standing like a tree, imagining my spine as a plumb line with my coccyx as the weight, even hanging from a golden string from the ceiling of my apartment. Then Taya climbed out of my bed where she had been napping and crossed in front of me on the way to her room. I got a sudden flash and decided to try it.

I imagined that I was wearing something like a diaper and that it was full of stones. I continued to deepen the feeling sense of the visualization. Suddenly I felt a warm current running up my back. At the same time my feet felt more firmly planted than before. I realized that I was experiencing a sense of rootedness that I had never known. With such an effortless alignment, I was able to stand for more than forty-five minutes. At the end of the exercise, I felt completely relaxed. I continued to practice this way for the rest of the days before class.

The next week we began the class as usual. After we had been standing only a few minutes, my friend's teacher came over to me. He looked surprised. "What did you do this week?"

I told him that I had changed the way I did standing meditation. That Taya had inspired me to stand with a different picture in my mind. I explained my image with the rocks.

He began laughing and slapping his thigh. "Very good. You give me a good idea. A secret teaching."

I wondered what exactly I had taught him, but I was about to find out.

"I have a new idea," he told the group. "When you do standing meditation this week, you stand like a baby with a big diaper. Diaper is full of shit. So heavy it weighs you down so you can hardly walk. This is a very good image for helping you to find roots and stand good. You do this every day for thirty minutes."

"But," said a student, "I find that image distasteful. I prefer to think of myself as a tree, stretching my branches to the sky."

"That's your problem. You're always reaching up, but you're not connected to the ground. That may be pretty, but it's not chi.

"When your pants are full of shit, that keeps you down. Then you understand: not pretty, just chi!

"Look at Linda," he added playfully. "She's full of shit this morning!" He turned and gave me a wink.

"I just follow the example of my great teacher," I said back playfully.

He came and slapped me on the back. "Good! Good! Finally you understand!"

Exercises

A STANDING (OR SITTING) MEDITATION

One time I asked my chi kung teacher: "If I have time to do only one exercise, what should I do?" Without hesitation he answered, "Just stand." He was referring to the standing meditation that we practiced at the beginning of each class. This kind of meditation, which is known by various names, such as Standing Like a Tree or Standing Like a Pillar Holding Up the Sky, is one of the most fundamental chi kung exercises.

Standing meditation helps to release a great deal of tension by allowing it to flow downward through the body into the earth. It also helps to give a strong sense of being grounded. But it does take time to learn. Please be patient. Begin with three to five minutes of standing, but practice consistently. As time goes by, you will know how much standing is appropriate for you.

This meditation can also be performed sitting on a chair, either in part or in its entirety. You may also begin by standing and then sit when you are tired. Just move slowly between the two positions.

Standing Posture

Begin by standing with your feet shoulder width apart, the toes pointing straight ahead. You may keep your eyes open or closed, whichever feels most comfortable. The knees are slightly bent. Your weight is centered over the middle of the feet. The rump is hanging downward as you slightly tuck your pelvis forward. Imagine that you are suspended from above by a string attached to the middle of your head. Your chin is pulled in a little, but not so far as to cause any tension in the chin or neck. Your hands are hanging slightly away from the body, as if you were holding your own closed fist under each arm. The hands are somewhat rounded, with the palms pointing toward your legs. In general, the upper body should have a light and long feeling, supported by a strong base in the legs.

After a few minutes, bring your hands to the front of your body and lay them on your abdomen. The thumbs are resting over the navel; the index fingers are touching.

Sitting on a Chair

If you are sitting on a chair, make sure that your feet are comfortably in contact with the floor. Your thighs should be as parallel to the floor as possible. If you are tall, you may need to sit on a cushion. If you are short, you may need to put something under your feet.

A straight-backed, flat-bottomed chair is best. If possible, sit forward on the chair. If you need to use the chair back to lean against, then place a cushion to support your back so that you do not lean too much.

Place the hands on the abdomen in the way described above.

The Breath As Anchor

In this meditation we use the breath as an anchor for our attention. Feel each in-breath and out-breath as precisely and carefully as you can. Stay in touch with the very physical sense of breathing. Let the breath come and go exactly the way it is. Do not try to change in it any way. Stand at least two minutes this way, with the hands resting on the abdomen.

When you feel ready, let your attention expand to take in the entire body. Sense your whole body, from head to toe. Then begin to move your awareness through the body, beginning at the top of the head. Think of your awareness like an elevator that is slowly lowering floor by floor. With each out-breath you release any tension as the awareness sinks downward. Be very gentle and do not force the breath in any way. When you reach your feet, let your awareness rest in the sensation of them in contact with the floor.

Feel how the body is relaxing with each breath yet maintaining its dignified upright posture. Feel the support of the ground or chair under you. You can let go of your weight and give it up to the earth or chair, knowing that you will be supported . . . that you will be held . . . that you can let go.

To end this exercise, whether you are standing or sitting, slide one hand over the other on your abdomen and rest for a few moments. Slowly open the eyes if they are closed.

Rub the hands together until they are warm and place them lightly over your eyes. Then give yourself a facial massage, massaging the forehead, cheeks, chin, and even the space between the nose and the lips. Stroke the front and back of your neck. Lay your hands on your chest and stroke several times downward. Stroke your arms, chest, back, and legs, also in a downward direction. Finish the massage by patting the body soundly, moving from the ankles upward to the head, both the back and front. Shake your hands as if they were wet to release any tension. Take a slow walk in the room or, better yet, in the fresh air.

A TREE IN A HEAVY STORM

At the end of the movement Preparation, you are standing with your feet parallel and shoulder width apart. Your arms are at your sides. Unlike the beginning of the posture, where your heels were touching, your base is now broader. Here the image we use is not so much that of being suspended from above as of standing like a tree, our roots reaching deep into the earth. Your lower body is the base; like a tree trunk it supports the weight of your upper body. Your head and arms are the branches of a tree, reaching ever upward, extending out from the solid base.

Widening and deepening is the movement of roots under the earth. As the tree grows higher, the roots spread more, anchoring the tree firmly to the ground. It's because of this that a tree can dance in the wind. Only when its roots are rotten does a tree lose its capacity to bend. At the first heavy puff, it topples.

Imagine that it is a warm sunny day and you are a tall, healthy tree enjoying this glorious day. Your leaves absorb the sun's rays, and the warmth spreads through your body. Your roots reach deep into the earth and draw water upward to nourish the leaves and branches. There is constant movement within you, and yet you stand immobile.

Imagine that a wind is beginning to blow. Raise your arms into the air and feel what it would be like for your branches to dance in the wind. At first the movements are light and playful. But as the wind turns into a storm, your movements become grander and more sweeping. Remember that you are a great tree with deep roots. So no matter how big your movements become, you remain rooted to the spot. Your feet stay planted right where they are.

After you have moved vigorously like a dancing willow in a spring breeze, imagine that the wind is slowly dying down. Come gradually to a halt. Stand quietly for a minute or two, observing any sensations. Allow the breath to come and go as it needs to. When you have a sense that the exercise is over, cover the lower stomach with your hands crossed over each other. End by doing the gentle massage described in the previous exercise.

Feeling our connection to the ground is something we emphasize over and over in t'ai chi. In the beginning, though, we are often up in our head, concerned with remembering and reproducing the movements. But with each step we take, with each day that goes by, our center sinks lower, whether we are aware of it or not.

A story I once read about the importance of trees in our own lives encouraged me to develop tree-imagery exercises for t'ai chi. The writer was talking about a tree in the garden of her family home as she was growing up. That tree was her special place; there she could hide from the world, curl up with a book or stroke her cat, who often scampered up to join her. More than the weather, the tree was a marker of the seasons and the passage of time. One day she returned home to find the tree had been cut down. She felt a great loss. But the memory of the tree was so strong it continued to inspire her for the rest of her life.

If you have a special tree in your life, call its image before your eyes during the standing meditation or when you do this exercise. In this way you bear witness to your life, and your t'ai chi form embodies and honors that journey.

The Heart of Practice

Unlike the forced effort we often apply to get things done, the effort required during the standing meditation is quite different. In meditation we apply a quiet determination. We make a decision to keep going—in a soft but firm way—and to keep returning to the breath when our attention wanders.

If you find that you are judging or commenting on yourself, either positively or negatively, then just note that, but do not get caught up in these thoughts. As soon as you notice that you are talking to yourself, then return to being aware of the breath.

You may notice from time to time that your mind wanders. You may find yourself caught up in a fantasy or a memory. Maybe you are planning or worrying about something. When you notice that your attention is no longer in the present moment, gently lead your attention back to the breath. Notice once again the sensations of breathing in and breathing out.

You may also notice sensations that disturb your ability to stay with the breath. You may feel some restlessness or irritation; perhaps an impulse to move will nag you. Do not try to suppress these thoughts or feelings, and do not begin a conversation with yourself. Just carefully guide your attention back to the breath.

Again and again and again.

Beginning

*B*eginning follows the movement Preparation. In fact, it is not quite correct to talk about one t'ai chi movement *following* another. *Flowing into one another* would be a more appropriate expression. The very nature of the t'ai chi movements is that they are seamless, yet each move has its own shape, texture, and quality. In the middle of doing the form, there is a sense of preciseness and attention to the moment, yet these moments happen moment after moment, continuously and infinitely. That is the paradox and mystery of t'ai chi. Doing the form offers us an opportunity to experience this intuitively.

At the start of Beginning you are standing with the feet parallel and shoulder width apart. The hands are pointing backward, retaining their slightly curved shape. Let the weight sink deep into your feet, as if you wanted to press down and touch the center of the earth.

Raise both hands at arm's length in front of the body to chest height. As you lift the arms, the fingers point toward the floor. The elbows are relaxed and hanging downward, rather than sticking out to the side.

When the hands are at chest height, raise the palms until they are parallel to the floor. To execute this movement, imagine that your fingers are balloons that fill with air. In other words, you do not lift the fingers so much as sense that your hands fill to take the shape of the next position: palms parallel to the floor and the fingers pointing forward.

Pull the hands back toward your body until they are about

a hand's length from the chest. Then raise your fingers until they are pointing upward. Again the action is aided through imagining that your hands are filling with air.

Do this movement slowly and with attention to the slight stretch in the palms. This action has the function of opening *lao gong*, an important acupuncture point in the middle of the palm. The opening of this point, according to the principles of Chinese medicine, allows us to draw in refreshing chi and to expell used chi. I personally like to think of this movement as a way to touch and feel the world around me, like an insect would use its antennae to sense and move through the environment.

End the movement by sliding the hands downward, as if your were brushing your fingers against an imaginary wall in front of you. Let the hands come to rest in the same position they started from.

Grand Master William C. C. Chen says that the t'ai chi movements are like waves in the ocean. Can we really say where a wave begins and where it ends? And yet a surfer can "catch a wave" and ride it for endless moments to the shore. It's all a matter of being in tune with the rhythm of the universe.

Think of t'ai chi as a kind of Taoist surfing, riding the waves and rhythms of the cosmos.

Surf's up!

6

"Shouting at a Bud Doesn't Make It Blossom More Quickly"

When I began t'ai chi, I was able to learn only the first half of the form before leaving New York for a cross-country trip. For more than three months I traveled with my husband and our baby daughter in a VW bus. When I finally returned to class, my former training partners had finished learning the form. I felt sad that I had fallen behind.

My teacher noticed that something was on my mind. One night she asked me to stay after class for a chat. After some prompting, I told her what was bothering me. She listened sympathetically, then asked me how I had trained while I was traveling.

Most of the time, I told her, we stayed in beautiful camp-sites in national parks. We were always up early. Usually I would go off to a quiet spot and practice for an hour or so. I did a series of warm-ups, then the form two or three times. Often I took sections and practiced them repeatedly, especially the ones I had trouble with. I also practiced sequences of front, side, and backward kicks, which helped me to build endurance and flexibility.

My teacher looked at me in amazement. "And you think that the other people are further along then you are?" she asked incredulously.

"Well, they know more of the form than I do," I said with a pout.

"They may know more of the form than you do, but you know more about the spirit of t'ai chi. With the kind of training you did, you prepared yourself for a lifetime of practice. You cultivated the true spirit of training that will allow you to learn anything, not just t'ai chi. Don't confuse true attainment with the appearance of it. And don't be such an ass!"

After more than twenty years, I know now how valuable this training was. But it was not easy in those days. There were quite a few mornings when I could not face, yet again, having to practice on my own. And there were many times when I finished my "short" form and wished I could go on, rather than having to begin at the beginning.

When you learn the form, there is a natural desire to want to move on as quickly as possible. Often the format of a weekly class creates the expectation of learning a new movement every session. We can easily get focused on the end result and rush through the process. Most disheartening, we think that if we do not learn the complete form, something is missing.

When you notice these kinds of thoughts coming up, take a moment to see what kind of effect they are having on your body and on your training spirit. One of the first things you might notice is that you become impatient, both with the teacher—who may not be moving as fast as you would like—and with anyone in the class who seems to be slowing things down. You may also notice that your speed increases in doing the form; when you practice in a group, you're always ahead of the others. If you could see yourself, you would also notice that the movements are not as full as they once were. Everything is being compromised in the name of speed.

Practicing t'ai chi is an opportunity to step out of the addiction to getting the most done in the least amount of time. Because learning t'ai chi in a slow, steady manner is such a contrast to the way we normally do things, it can feel at first as if something is wrong. But it is not wrong, just different.

Think of your t'ai chi form as a seed you have planted in the garden of life. Each seed has its own time schedule. Of course, there are many techniques for speeding up the growth process, including artificial light and greenhouses. And yet, as every gardener knows, flowers and plants produced under these conditions are not hardy. The moment they leave the greenhouse they begin to die, living only long enough to get sold and be kept at home for a few days.

Experienced t'ai chi practitioners (known as "players") may learn a form quickly, but they will go home and spend many months practicing and deepening their understanding. There is no shortcut that will substitute for the kind of practice time that will cause your form to flower.

"Shouting at a bud does not make a flower blossom more quickly," writes vipassana meditation teacher Christina Feldman, in *The Quest of the Warrior Woman*.[1] Racing through the t'ai chi form doesn't do it either.

7
Expectations

When I first began to practice Zen in 1979, I threw myself into it as much as possible. It was never easy to get away to the Zen center, but Friday evenings were especially tough because I was working the all-night shift as a copy editor at a national news magazine. My boss, though herself not a meditator, sensed my urgency. I will always be grateful to her for letting me take a long dinner break to sit quietly on a cushion for a couple of hours.

It was like running a marathon on those Friday evenings. I would dash out of the huge skyscraper where my office was located, hail a cab, and ask to be driven as fast as possible to the Zen center twenty blocks away. Two hours later, I'd jump back into a cab and race back to work. From then until eight the next morning, stories about war, poverty, stock markets, major medical discoveries, murder, celebrity life, earthquakes, all passed over my desk. The hours I had spent earlier in zazen (sitting meditation) helped to balance the sense of chaos and universal crisis that erupted in the world.

As time went on I joined the jukai class at the center, which was to prepare me to receive the precepts and become a lay Buddhist. I also went several times to the center's beautiful monastery in the countryside. And yet, for all this activity, I did not take part in the heart of Zen practice: I never had dokusan, or a private interview, with the teacher. It wasn't an oversight. I avoided it like the plague. It was not difficult because dokusan took place only on certain evenings or during sesshin, the intensive silent retreats that lasted anywhere from one day to an entire week. Since I purposely did not go to them, I never met the teacher face-to-face.

I was terrified to go to dokusan. First, I was afraid of the teacher, who was a very traditional Japanese Rinzai monk who embodied what I thought of as samurai Zen. Though I was not exactly timid, I was completely intimidated by his sternness, his ability to electrify me with his occasional eruptions in the zendo (the meditation hall), and his strict observation of the form.

But I was more afraid of not knowing what to do or say when I did meet him. I didn't know anything about the proper etiquette or what to talk about. I didn't have robes or know how to bow properly. I wasn't working on koans, didn't know much about Zen history, didn't know much of anything about Zen. In short, I was afraid of being found out, of appearing inadequate, ill-prepared, and incompetent. Others had described dokusan as being so intimate. That scared me the most. I didn't want to be intimate. I wanted to hide in anonymity, take what I needed—and run.

I was not at all prepared when I finally met a Zen teacher face-to-face. It happened in 1984 in Europe when I was visiting a t'ai chi friend whose husband was studying Zen with an American teacher. One Sunday morning he casually asked if I would like to go with him to the zendo to meet his teacher. I jumped out of the chair and ran to get my coat.

We joined a small group of people who were already

sitting zazen in the living room of a suburban apartment. The smell of incense and the sight of the altar awoke a deep sense of longing in me, as if I had found something that I had lost a long time ago. As the gong sounded, tears slid down my cheeks.

After the first sitting, the teacher stood up and left the room. A second period began, and I was soon deep in zazen. Suddenly I felt a tap on my shoulder. I turned to see my friend signaling that I should follow him. We walked down the hall and he pointed to a closed door. He indicated I should go in and then left immediately.

I opened the door and saw the teacher sitting on the floor. He said cheerily, "Hello. Come on in!"

There was a cushion and mat in front of him. He pointed to them: "Have a seat." I sat down casually. "Where are you from?" he began. We talked for about ten minutes about all the things two Americans talk about when they live abroad. We compared notes about the food, housing, raising kids in Europe, learning the customs, shopping in a foreign language. "Well, next time you're here, you're welcome to come back," he said as our conversation drew to a close. I got up, turned at the door to wave good-bye, and left. As I was walked down the hall to the living room, I thought, "That was nice of him to welcome me like that."

Everyone was still sitting zazen, so I joined them. As I entered the room, the person sitting next to me got up and went down the hall. A little bell rang; she bowed at the door and entered the room where I had just been. The door closed with a light click.

Suddenly a thought shot through me. "That was dokusan!" I nearly fell off my cushion. I kept repeating over and over to myself, "I don't believe it! I just don't believe it!" A deep laugh began to rumble at the core of my being. It spread through my entire body like shock waves, touching every part of me. Through it all I managed to sit erect and keep still.

So simple.

But until the moment it actually happened, meeting the teacher seemed like the most difficult thing in the world.

It is easy to create the same kind of psychological hurdles about learning t'ai chi as I did about meeting the teacher. They take many forms, but in the end they all have some-thing to do with expectations.

In my own case, I had many wonderful expectations when I first began to study t'ai chi. I had visions of flowing in dreamlike movements, sensing peace and harmony all around me. I was sure that I would experience the secret of the Taoist masters. As I watched my teacher move with ele-gance and muted power, I became even more excited. But that excitement soon turned into frustration and disappoint-ment as I struggled to learn the two short movements she so patiently repeated in the first class. At the end of the class, I was sure of only one thing: either my expectations had to go out the door or I did. I chose to stay.

Over and over during the many years that I have been teaching, I watch my own students arrive at their first class with the same expectations that I had. They seek to be more peaceful, to improve their balance, to learn something that will help them cope with stress. Their longing is so great that many hope to reap the benefits of t'ai chi from the moment they begin to learn the form. In this mode of wishful thinking, they often ignore common sense. No one would expect to be a great pianist after one lesson, and yet many beginning t'ai chi students believe that after a short class they will be able to move with the grace and effortlessness of a long-time practitioner.

Not seeing into the nature of our expectations can be a great barrier in t'ai chi practice. In severe life circumstances, it can be fatal. It takes maturity, faith, and trust to finally see how we create obstacles through holding on to expectations—about t'ai chi or anything else. It takes the same mettle to see ourselves as we are: tender and trusting, fearful and protective, teary and furious, full of all the wonderful nuances of being human.

If there's any good in having expectations, it is because of the relief that comes when we see how much pain they cause and how free we can be when we don't burden ourselves with them. When we learn to recognize our expectations for what they are, the world becomes a much richer place, even as we let go of expecting it to give us anything.

8
Just Keep Going

In his book *Body Mechanics of T'ai Chi Chuan*, Grand Master William C. C. Chen explains how he practiced as a young man:

> After my daily practice of the T'ai Chi Chuan forms, I broke down the form into a set of 4 or 5 movements to use as fighting techniques. I spent an additional hour to train in these techniques and repeated each of them 200 to 500 times in slow motion and with relaxation. This allowed me to focus my mind on the inner energy flow, coordinated with the outer action. Once I had repeated each technique 5000 times or more, the conditioning of these techniques reached a satisfactory level of performance in slow motion as well as at full speed. I then went on to the next set of movements, and so on.[1]

When I read this to beginning students, they are often intimidated. "I could never do that," they say. "I'm not disciplined enough. And besides, I don't have Master Chen's ability."

But discipline or mastery is not the issue. The real issue for many students is that the moment they think about practicing, all sorts of voices come up that try to talk them out of it. These voices usually have something negative to say. "You'll never be able to learn all those movements, so why bother?" says one. Another says, "Just take care of the laundry, the food shopping, and cleaning the house. Then you can begin." A third voice says, "You're not calm enough to practice. Wait until you feel more peaceful."

When we are training together with others, or in class, these voices don't appear. Practicing together gives the feeling of being in community, which can be very nourishing. Also, the dynamics of being in a group carry us along. Both positive and negative, they function as a motor and keep us on the path.

So what do you do when you want to practice and the voices begin their litany? It's not a good idea to fight them. When we do, we actually give them more energy as well as creating a situation in which we are at war with ourselves.

We should not struggle with these voices, but we don't have to listen to them either! We can quiet them by simply practicing in spite of everything. Just don't listen when a voice says you have to feel like practicing, that you have to feel you are getting something, that you should be perfect. The most effective way to practice is to just practice.

Just keep going!

To just keep going is to connect to the most natural rhythms of life. The sun just rises, the wind just blows, the seasons just change. Yet we have such great difficulty in just keeping going. Why, for example, do we set the limitation that before we can go on, we want our house, our life, and all our relationships in order—and the bank account topped up? That's just not possible. And yet each time we postpone practicing until we have taken care of all the things that suddenly became so important, we are trying to do the impossible. It becomes a rat race, a vicious circle, a trap without a way out.

When you catch yourself thinking, "I should practice," then just keep going. Stand up and do the form. No matter where you are, what time of day it is, whether you've got your training clothes on or not, are wearing the right shoes, have done the right warm-ups, have eaten the right meal, or whatever. As you do the form, all these preoccupations fall away and you fall into practice in spite of yourself. Try it right now! Put down this book and stand up and do the form or any exercise that lasts for at least ten minutes. . . .

What did you learn? Take a moment to be in touch with that. And if you skipped over this last suggestion, then take a moment to be with that.

Some time ago a woman shared with me her own discovery of what it means to just keep going. When she began t'ai chi, she told me, she had no space at home to practice. Her school offered her the keys to a satellite center near where she lived on the condition that she set up early morning practice sessions—and be there every weekday so that other students could train there too.

An announcement was made in the school's newsletter about the new practice hours. The woman waited expectantly the next Monday after the newsletter appeared, but nobody came. Most mornings were the same. Once in a while someone turned up, and she hoped he or she would stay. But the person usually stopped coming. When I last saw her, this had been going on for eight months.

"Every morning I begin all over again," she told me. "The only difference from when I first started practicing here is that I'm not waiting for anyone to come anymore. If they do, I'm happy to have someone to practice with. If no one comes, I just keep going."

9

On Your Own: Practicing Alone

The hardest thing about learning the form in the beginning is not the difficulty in remembering the movements. Finding twenty minutes for yourself during the day to practice alone—that can feel like the hardest thing in the world.

There are many reasons why it is so difficult. A big one is that we are taught to value everyone and everything else except ourselves. We feel we should be doing something for our family, our company, or society. Taking time for ourselves only makes us feel guilty. Or we think that to take time for ourselves is to waste time. Either way we are trapped in a cycle that puts everything and everyone else first.

Developing the routine of practicing alone in class helps to work with this issue. It is one of the reasons why, after I teach a new move, I always ask my students to practice it individually for ten minutes. Then I leave the room. Leaving them alone is the only way I know to encourage them to trust themselves to practice on their own. Without the confidence of having done it alone in class, it's so easy to talk ourselves out of practicing when we go home. When we confirm in class that we are capable of working alone, it supports us when we wake up the next morning and want to train.

The first time I leave a new group alone, there is usually some minor panic. Sometimes a student tells me that she is afraid to practice on her own. "I don't want to do anything wrong," she says. But in actuality, it is much more difficult to work on the form when we have not practiced than it is to adjust something that is off. Whether we can correctly reproduce a movement is not the issue when we are first learning it. The most important thing is to give the body the experience of moving in the t'ai chi mode.

I once heard a poignant story about the value of practicing alone—in class and at home. It concerns a couple who spent eight years living and working in Malaysia. Soon after arriving, they joined a t'ai chi class near their home. Every morning, seven days a week, they participated in the class. There was no need to practice outside the group because they went almost every day. When they retired back to England, they vowed that whatever else changed, they would continue to practice t'ai chi every morning.

The very first day after they resettled back home, they rose early and went to the park. It felt lonely at first, because unlike in Malaysia, where the parks were full of people early in the morning, their park was almost empty. Still, they took their positions and began to do the form. Halfway through it, they stopped dead in their tracks. Neither of them could remember the rest of the form! Bits and pieces came floating back, but they could not put them together without great effort. For the first time in their t'ai chi practice they found themselves doing the moves over and over, trying to remember what came next.

After some weeks, with a great deal off effort, they managed to do the whole form, but it felt very strange and unfamiliar. The sense of comfort and security with which they had practiced before was gone. They continued to train for several months until their form felt smooth again. Six months later they agreed to teach t'ai chi to the many friends and relatives who had asked to learn with them. They taught the way their teacher did, but with one difference: they included a session within each class where the students had to practice on their own.

Each time you learn a new move of the form, there will be only one opportunity when you practice it alone for the first time, only one time when you can experience this mixture of fright and wonder. These moments are precious. We can run away from them by not practicing alone and thus resign ourselves to a life of mimicry of someone else's t'ai chi. Or we can greet them with wonder and open arms, thus laying the groundwork for a t'ai chi practice that will always reflect from our own center.

10
The Miracle of Mindfulness

Mindfulness meditation is a Buddhist practice that helps calm and center the mind. Jon Kabat-Zinn, the founder of the Stress Reduction Clinic at the University of Massachusetts Memorial Medical Center in Worcester, Massachusetts, defines mindfulness as "paying attention on purpose in the moment." In practicing mindfulness, we learn to watch our mind with a certain detachment. It's not a cold distancing but a willingness to let everything come up and be present, neither getting caught up in our thoughts nor trying to suppress them. Mindfulness meditation is a practice, or exercise, because the quality of being awake and aware that characterizes it needs to be trained. Our minds are so full of inner dialogue, so busy with planning, remembering, analyzing, blaming, or explaining, that we rarely come to this quiet but present state of mind. But as we continue to practice, we can experience times when the cycle of habitual thinking is broken and we are fresh, alive, and completely present in the now. You know those moments: it can be watching the swallows circle above the market square or following your child's efforts as he builds sand castles to challenge the great ocean's tides.

Mindfulness is about being fully awake in our lives. It is

about experiencing each moment in all its vitality, in all its reality, in its joys and sorrows, exactly as it is. When we rest in the moment, we have an opportunity to be at home in our bodies, neither fighting nor pushing nor rejecting ourselves. We learn to take care and to give care in a wholesome, balanced, and trusting way. As we experience the path of mindfulness, we connect to the capacity of each of us to mobilize our own resources for coping, for healing, and for growing.

One skillful way to begin mindfulness practice is by attending to the breath. First we direct our attention either to the top of the lip, to the bottom of the nose, or to the abdomen. As we breathe we stay with the physical sensation of movement in those areas. We feel the air moving over the lip or through the nasal passage. If we are paying attention to the abdomen, then we sense the rise and fall of our stomach or torso. The goal is not to control the breath but to feel the physical sensations as the body moves.

As the practice deepens, you can more finely observe the breath by sensing its different qualities. A breath can be long, short, cool, warm, flowing, choppy, thin, wide, and so on. Using the breath as an anchor to keep yourself in the present moment, you can reach deeper and deeper levels of subtlety about the nature of breath—and about yourself.

Applying the lessons of mindfulness meditation to t'ai chi practice is really to discover the heart of t'ai chi as meditation in movement. I use t'ai chi as a mindfulness practice by substituting awareness of the body in movement for awareness of the breath. I encourage students to feel the sensations in their body as they do the form. For example, we might go through the form paying careful attention to what we sense in the feet as we shift our weight and take a step, feeling every part of the foot touching the floor. We do sessions sensing the back, registering its full expanse rather than just being focused on the front of the body as we usually are.

Paying attention to our sensations keeps us focused in the moment. Being fully present in each part of the form also helps to break the obsession of wanting to rush through it. The following incident is a typical example of how this might come up in class:

Joe calls me over to where he is practicing a move he learned the week before. "I'm confused about a move. Can you help me?" "Show me," I say. Because Joe doesn't know the form well, he has to back up a few moves to find the place where he is having trouble. He rushes through the form to get to the place where he is having a problem.

"Okay," he says, "here's where my problem begins."

"Just here?" I ask as innocently as possible.

"Nah, forget what you just saw . . . this part, here! This is where the problem is!"

"The problem lies as much in what comes before as here," I say quietly. "You're pushing through the form. While you are doing one movement, your mind is in the next." An exasperated look comes over Joe's face.

"Go back to the beginning of this section and do the form with the kind of moment-to-moment attention we've been practicing," I encourage him. "See what happens."

It takes time and practice to learn how to put the brakes on. But in time, if we work at it, we learn to have a more relaxed attitude about the whole thing. Instead of a manic drive to master the form, there's a curiosity to discover the form again in each moment.

Practicing t'ai chi as a mindfulness meditation also helps us to work with a slow-to-grow tendency that can certainly undermine our motivation to practice: feeling bored.

Boredom is something that comes up at different stages of t'ai chi practice. For example, we often get bored repeating a move over and over. We assume we have mastered the exercise. But in fact we have allowed ourselves to be lulled into a kind of drowsiness where we have lost the capacity to see the freshness in each repetition.

When I feel bored while practicing t'ai chi, I know that I've lost the capacity to be awake in that moment. It may mean I need to take a rest, to come to terms with my frustration, or both. In any case, I know that I must again awaken that quality of attention that transforms even repetitive operations into moments that sparkle with uniqueness.

After I began practicing Zen meditation, I decided to bring that quality of mindfulness into my t'ai chi practice. I began by paying careful attention to each part of my body as I did the form: the sensation in my hand or my foot, the weight of my arm, the length of my step. Sometimes I could focus only for a few moments; gradually the time increased. I was amazed at the richness within even one movement. It was like being with an old friend who constantly surprised me.

I also began to look at how boredom affected my life, specifically my tendency to have several projects cooking at once. At any one time, some projects were on a high flame, some were simmering on the back burner. By the time the food was cooked in the front, I had lost interest in it. I wouldn't even taste it but would immediately turn my attention to the pot behind it. In this way there was always something cooking. Always another project waiting.

I applied what I had learned from t'ai chi practice and began to focus on one project at a time. I paid attention to the point where boredom began. And then I noticed it wasn't boredom at all. That was just a name I gave to a set of emotions that I really didn't want to call by its true name. I became bored when it seemed that I was going to have to add one last bit of effort to be successful. I was attached to having something going on, not to finishing it. Having a project gave my life meaning. I acknowledged for the first time that I was addicted to busyness because I was afraid of empty moments.

The next time you feel bored when practicing t'ai chi, take a moment to be with whatever feelings are coming up. Just let the images or feelings flow. Adopt an attitude of quiet watching, letting go of any tendency that wants to do something or push in one direction or the other. This may take time, while the habits of thinking and doing are so ingrained. It may help just to get in touch with your breath, if you are standing quietly. If you are doing the form, then just move through the movements with a commitment to looking . . . looking . . . looking.

When you recognize boredom in the form for what it is, you can use the momentum of that insight to bring the quality of mindfulness to your practice—and to your life. If you don't try to get rid of the boredom by doing something "interesting," it well tell you a lot about what is going on. Whatever happens, we will experience what Vietnamese Zen master Thich Nhat Hanh calls "the miracle of mindfulness."

11

Give Yourself a Present

"Come quick! I need your help in the cake-decorating department." I looked incredulously at the Japanese monk over the mountain of loaves of bread I was holding. I had signed up for a samu sesshin (where work is practiced as meditation) at the Zen Community of New York and had immediately been put to work in the bakery in Yonkers. We rose early for zazen but spent most of the day amid cakes, cookies, bread, and other delectables the Zen bakery was growing famous for. We must have worked at least twelve hours on Saturday, taking short breaks that were over before they began. The work was exhausting, but even more wearing was the adjustment to the scale of things in a commercial bakery. Everything was huge. The ovens, the mixers, the bread pans. I had always enjoyed baking when I had the time. But this was serious stuff, and the jaws of the mammoth ovens scared me.

By the end of Saturday I had gotten into the rhythm of things and could negotiate my way around the place. And I also had the answers to two questions that had only mildly troubled me. First, I understood why there had been no charge for the sesshin. And second, I understood why I was the only one who had signed up for it.

On Sunday I was asked to assist the head cake maker. As I entered the kitchen where he worked, I found the Zen monk, Yoshi, standing over a huge cake with a pastry decorator in his hands. He was embellishing the cake with exquisite designs. I knew there was only icing in the thing he was squeezing, but the roses, leaves, and other beautiful objects that emerged from it made it clear that here was a magician/artist at work. Yoshi moved around the table as if he were a master ballroom dancer. And like a dancer, he only had eyes for the piece of cake in front of him.

He put me to work cleaning up the mess that was all around him. After I had finished, he asked me to assist him by peeling off decorations that were prebaked and which he used as the base for more complicated designs. We spent several hours working in this manner. Though I always said I had no art talent, this work brought me back to the joy of creation that I had experienced in an eighth-grade pottery class. I still had the cherished, lopsided pot that I had made by coiling strands of clay on top of each other.

It was getting toward 3:00 P.M. on Sunday. The sesshin was scheduled to end around 4:30. The phone rang and Yoshi answered it. After he put down the receiver, he had a serious look on his face.

"We've got a problem," he announced. "You've got to help me."

"What can I do?" I asked.

"That was the office. One of our most important customers needs a cake this afternoon at 4:30. He forgot to order it for a birthday party tonight. He wants it decorated with the works!"

"What's the problem? You can give him the one you just did."

"No, I can't. That's for another customer who is already waiting in the office to pick it up." He scratched his head and looked about him. He really looked worried.

"I'll be right back," he said in a rush. "I've got to bring this cake out front anyway."

I busied myself cleaning up the by now inevitable mess. Suddenly Yoshi burst through the door, holding a large undecorated cake in his hands. He set it down on the table.

"All hell is breaking loose!" he said anxiously. "There's a problem with the batch of cookies for our big client downtown. I've got to go and take care of it. You've got to decorate this cake and have it ready at 4:30 for the guy to pick up."

He was out the door before my mouth fully dropped open. I stared at the swinging door that was the only trace of him.

"No way!" I shouted in the direction he had disappeared. "It's impossible. I can't do it! There's no way I can decorate this cake!"

I paced the room for several minutes, frantically wondering what to do. "I've got to tell him to find someone else!" But even as I uttered the words, I knew it was hopeless. The only other person who could have done it had gone home. There was only a skeleton crew finishing up some other work. I felt terrible, mostly because I was letting the bakery and Yoshi down. An important customer would be disappointed, and I would be the cause of his taking his business elsewhere.

My back was up against one big wall. I approached the table, letting my eyes run over everything for a few moments. I picked up the icer, took a deep breath, and began squeezing.

I don't know where the time went, but I did a lot of squeezing in that hour. After a while I lost myself in the work. The fear that I wasn't artistic enough, that it would be a mess, also faded away. I even felt some satisfaction as I learned to squeeze with just the right pressure so that drops looked like drops and not squashed mud pies. I got into color combinations, doodling lines, a nifty lettering for "Happy Birthday." When I finished, I sat back with pride, satisfaction, and a quiet sense of wonder. The decorating could certainly qualify for the label of unusual, perhaps unusual and beautiful.

Yoshi burst through the door at 4:25. "Is it ready?" he asked excitedly.

"Voilà! Regardez, s'il vous plaît!" I stepped back so he could get a full view of my masterpiece.

He approached the table slowly, then moved around it, viewing the cake from all angles. For a moment I panicked. From the viewpoint of a master decorator, it was probably a mess, a kitsch combination of bizarre forms.

But a slow smile spread across his face. He turned and said sincerely, "It's wonderful! You did a good job. They'll love it!"

Tears sprang to my eyes. I felt deeply honored.

Yoshi began wrapping up the cake, leaving me to wipe my eyes and set myself right again. He tied several ribbons around it and made quite a show of doing them up. When he finished, he picked up the cake in both hands. He turned and walked toward me, then stopped.

He handed the cake to me. "Happy birthday, Linda!" he said, with a smile all over his face and deep into his eyes. In a moment he was out the door again.

Many people begin t'ai chi with the same attitude I had about my ability to decorate the cake. They deeply appreciate the beauty of the form, but at the same time they think they will never be capable of performing such beauty themselves.

In beginning t'ai chi, or in beginning anything that causes your heart to sing and makes you want to study it, think of it as an opportunity to give yourself a present, a very special treat. Sometimes it's difficult to joyfully give ourselves something because we're often judging, measuring, or comparing ourselves with others. When you find you are making judgments about yourself, be aware of that, but then go beyond it. Connect to that part of you that felt the wish to bring such beauty into your life. Honor your desire to practice, to follow a path with heart—and then just keep going. And if it helps, then when you finish your form, or whatever your task is, walk over to a mirror and say to yourself, "This one's for you, kid! Happy birthday!"

Exercises

I Am a Camera: Moving from the Center

This exercise helps us to experience one of the most important t'ai chi principles: moving from our center. This center is called the *tan tien* in Chinese, which is translated in English as the "cinnabar field." This center of our vital or life energy is said to lie approximately three fingers' width beneath the navel at a point about one inch deep within the body. When all our movements originate from this center, we feel stable, grounded, and yet free to move with lightness and agility.

The Basic Exercise

Begin by doing the standing meditation described on page 31. As you stand with your hands on the abdomen (thumbs over the navel and index fingers touching), guide your awareness to the open area formed by the meeting of your fingers and your thumbs. As you inhale, feel as if the air is moving down to this area. As you exhale, feel the breath flow from there and out of the body.

Do not force the breath to be either long or deep. Continue breathing in this way for at least two minutes.

Now imagine that the point between your fingers and thumbs is the lens of a video camera. Your goal is to shoot a panoramic picture in a 180-degree angle. Slowly turn your body to the right as far as is comfortable. It is helpful to relax and sink into the groin as if you were going to turn and sit down.

Now slowly film from right to left in a steady motion, just

as you would if you were holding a camera; you want the picture to be as smooth as possible.

When you reach as far left as you can go, then slowly scan back to the right. Let the hands be relaxed and do not hunch the shoulders. If you notice that you are doing so, then roll your shoulders a few times and let them sink again.

When you have a sense that all is flowing smoothly, you might try coordinating the turning with the breath. Beginning at the farthest point to the right, breathe in as you scan left. Let the speed of scanning comfortably match the rhythm of your breathing.

When you reach the farthest point left, pause for a few seconds. As you move right, breathe out. There should always be a slight pause between the out-breath and the in-breath or vice versa to avoid dizziness. Continue the scanning for as long as you feel comfortable, but for a minimum of three minutes.

Many people do the exercise with their eyes open. However, others enjoy closing their eyes. Experiment with both ways and explore the differences between the two.

Placing the hands on the abdomen helps you to center the mind there. But you may find that you suddenly go on automatic pilot, which means doing the exercise but thinking about something else. If you find that to be the case, just guide your awareness back to the physical sensation of the space between your fingers and thumbs.

When you are ready to terminate the exercise, slowly come to a halt in the middle. Slide one hand over the other and end with the body massage as described on page 33.

Variation 1

If you know a t'ai chi form or a part of one, then do it immediately after the camera exercise without doing the closing massage. Keep your awareness centered in the abdomen. In certain parts of the form it may be more difficult than others, such as when we do expansive arm movements. At those times, pay extra attention to staying in your center. End the form with your hands placed on the abdomen, and then close with the massage.

Variation 2

It's also possible to do I Am a Camera while moving about the room. You do not turn from side to side, as in the stationary exercise, but move with a steady awareness in your center. Always start by doing the stationary exercise a few times and then begin walking. Slowly. At first, walk in straight lines backward and forward. When you are able to stay focused in your center, try turning and walking in various directions. You can also experiment with different speeds.

Variation 3

It can be quite a lot of fun to do Variation 2 with music. Anything with a strong regular beat is appropriate. I sometimes use the track "Above the Wailing Wall" from the album *The Dreams of Children* by Shadowfax. Develop any patterns you wish. Sometimes group members will begin dancing together, all the while moving from the center.

Just be sure to begin and end in stillness. And don't forget the closing massage.

PICK UP THE STRANDS

When you first learn a t'ai chi movement and go home to practice, you often forget some or all of the very last movement that you learned. Don't give up! Your body knows the movement, or at least some of it. Here is a way that you can work with this situation.

Go back to the beginning of the movement where you are stuck. Stand quietly for a moment with your arms at your sides. Stand with a gentle attention and a sense of your body as it is in that moment. Don't force yourself to remember anything.

When you feel quiet, begin the movement again. Try to have an attitude of open expectancy rather than fierce concentration. If you get stuck at a point and don't know what comes next, then stand for some moments in that position. If you begin to move, don't censor the movement. Even if it is not quite right, there might be something about it that helps you to remember the movement. Wait until you finish before making a decision about what to keep and what to let go of.

If nothing at all comes to mind, then begin the movement again. As you get closer to the part that you forgot, you will find a certain apprehension, as if you were about to enter the unknown. Don't plunge ahead and don't pull yourself back. Just keep going.

Even if you don't remember the move, this way of working will be very helpful. It trains a general attentiveness and encourages us to pay attention to our body sensations. It also helps us to become more intimate with all our movements and with a particular movement, despite its holes. Because you have been deeply engaged in practicing, the moment you see the movement again in class, something clicks into place. Rather than feeling as if you were meeting someone for the first time, it will be like recognizing someone you don't know very well but with whom you have spent happy times. Enjoy the reunion!

Forgetting a move is like dropping a strand of wool as you

knit. Pick up the strand again and continue working. You will soon have a most wonderful work of art.

The Heart of Practice

We often set up a competition with ourselves when we do such exercises. The moment we notice we are not focusing on the breath or have forgotten a movement, we think we have failed at the exercise. But in fact, the moment we notice we are not attending to the breath or that we've lost our place, we are directly present in the moment again.

Whatever thoughts come up, just let them come and let them go. Don't get caught up in the story line. This will, however, happen, but when you notice it, then return your attention to the scanning, to the breath, or to the exercise at hand.

Both these exercises also have something to teach us about being focused inward and yet not cutting ourselves off from the world. It's very similar to doing meditation with our eyes slightly open rather than closed. We tend to want to close them because we want to shut out distraction or unpleasant things. But meditation is not about shutting ourselves off from the world. It is about being present in our life and appreciating it—in the midst of everything that is going on.

Ward-Off

Ward-Off Left is the third movement of the t'ai chi form that I practice. The very next movement is Ward-Off Right, which has a similar function of repelling a blow, this time from the right direction. Begin Ward-Off Left by standing with your feet shoulder-width apart and parallel. Both arms are hanging at the side, with a bit of space under the arm. Your weight is in the middle of both feet. Then shift the weight almost completely onto the left leg. Next turn ninety degrees on the heel of the right foot; the torso will also turn toward the right. At the same time, lift the right hand and place it a shade above the right breast, as if it were sitting on top of a large beach ball. Also simultaneously, the left hand moves to sit in the area of the right groin, as if it were holding the ball from below.

Shift the weight 100 percent onto the right foot. Lift the left foot and set the heel down on the spot where the toes were before. Still holding the ball, shift the weight forward 70 percent onto the left foot. At this point turn the right foot 45 degrees toward the front and lift the left palm so that it points toward the solar plexus. At the same time, the right hand pushes down and toward the back, coming to rest next to the right leg with the palm pointing backward. Remember to keep the legs slightly bent at all times.

Shifting the weight is a critical process in t'ai chi. Many teachers have depicted it in various ways, but I find a description by Master Peter Ralston, author of *Cheng Hsin: The*

Principles of Effortless Power to be especially helpful. During a workshop he used the expression "to shift the weight under the floor." According to my understanding of this phrase, if we want to shift our weight backward and we are standing with the weight on the forward leg, then before we shift, we first sink the weight onto the forward leg. Then with the sense that something is moving under the floor, we move backward until our weight is, say, 90 percent on the back leg. Then we settle the weight on the back leg and sink down again. As we begin to move forward, we again imagine that we are shifting the weight under the floor to the front leg.

Since Ward-Off Left and Right are the first movements of the form where we take a step forward, we need to take time to discover how to do this in the most flowing but also stable way. Thinking in terms of shifting the weight under the floor helps us to avoid the rising up and loss of connection to the earth. Many students do lose it in the beginning, and thus in shifting they stand up and straighten the knees. Just keep thinking "Down, down, down!" Imagine that the soles of your feet are glued to the floor. In fact, your upper body from the waist up stays basically on the same level the whole time.

Often the step in Ward-Off Left or Right is taken in such a way that we stand far too narrow at the end of the movement. Although it may feel wide enough because one foot is in front of the other, this is deceiving. The space to pay attention to is the one between the inner sides of the feet. They must be shoulder-width apart. It is critical to spend a lot of time practicing this phase of the movement so that our body understands what the correct distance is.

The space between the left palm and the solar plexus is often too narrow. I encourage my students to think there is a large beach ball between their hand and their chest. Too often the ball gets smaller and smaller as the lesson progresses, as if it had sprung a leak. I ask them to keep checking in to their posture and especially to ask themselves whether they are too narrow or collapsed in their arm movements.

We tend to hide behind the t'ai chi movements, as if we were using our arms to protect us from the outside world rather than to extend into the space around us. The movements are not meant to separate us or create walls, but to allow us to extend in all directions of our life. To illustrate this, I like to show my students the drawing by Leonardo da Vinci where a man is standing with his arms outstretched to the side and his legs in a wide V. His head, hands, and feet are all touching the circumference of a circle. I ask them to imagine a circle like Leonardo's around their own body. We experiment with reaching out in different directions to feel the width and breadth of this imaginary circle of power.

Rather then hiding within the form, I encourage my students to let the form be full and present in their bodies, just as I hope it will help them to feel full and present in their lives. If I had to express it in words, I would say the posture at the end of Ward-Off Left is saying, "Hello. Here I am!"

And the universe answers, "Welcome!"

12
Take a Giant Step

$\mathcal{E}$mily had been studying t'ai chi with me for more than three years. One day I watched her do the form. As usual, whenever she took a step, her stance ended up very narrow. She resembled a pyramid trying to stand on its point rather than on its base. I don't know how many times in the past I had reminded her to take a wider step, but she rarely translated my request into action.

Something in me snapped. I walked over and asked her to start the form from the beginning. At the moment she lifted her foot to take a step, I grabbed it. "Like this," I said, and set it down wider than she would have done on her own.

The look on her face was one of pure astonishment. "So wide!" she exclaimed in disbelief. She remained still for a moment, absorbing the new impressions that came with standing wider than she was used to. Then she continued on to the next move. Again, just as she was about to set her foot down, I moved it more to the right. She shook her head: "I don't believe it!"

We finished the form in exactly the same way. Sometimes I actually held her foot, sometimes I just said "Wider!" when she was about to set it down. It took well over thirty minutes to do the form, which normally takes from seven to ten minutes. By the time she finished, Emily was tired and beads of sweat had gathered on her brow.

We stood staring at each other, neither of us sure what to say. Finally Emily asked, "Do I have to practice like this from now on?"

"Yes," I said clearly. "Just like that."

"But it feels so strange. I feel I'm doing a completely different form."

"Any change we make in the form, no matter how big or small, feels like it changes the form completely," I said. "But you will be amazed how quickly the strange becomes familiar, if you practice regularly. The form will feel right to you this way, and the narrow steps you took before will feel off. You're leading your body to explore a new mode of being. It's a slow but very thorough process."

For the rest of the class, I worked individually with other students. Occasionally I glanced in Emily's direction. Usually I found her standing with one foot in midair, experimenting with where to set it down. Once she caught my eye and raised her foot even higher, as if she were a male dog relieving itself. "That one's for you!" she said.

I could understand her frustration and appreciate her playful gesture. It was certainly not an easy assignment that I had given her. I had asked her to take apart the form as she knew it and to relearn it. I had asked her to become conscious of what she had become unconscious about, to turn off the automatic pilot and become an active driver. And I had done it in a rather intrusive way.

Although I didn't plan it that way, the exercise with Emily became an experiment in conscious intervention. I had never so directly manipulated a student's form before—and never on such an extensive scale. If Emily had shaken me off at some point as a person with a dog tearing at the leg of her pants would do, I would have understood. But she didn't, and we kept going.

We both learned something from this exercise. As far as Emily was concerned, her form changed completely in the space of a few months. Previously she always seemed somewhat shaky in her postures, as if she would topple at any moment. Now she appeared firmly centered and rooted, as if she were a sphinx that remained immovable throughout time. And yet in the very next moment, she could move lightly and as freely as a cat on a hot tin roof.

I learned, or rather had confirmed, that a form correction in itself does nothing to change behavior permanently. Simply adjusting isolated movements by shifting a hand here or moving a foot there does not translate into learning that lasts. Unless the body has a chance to experience the change as a new mode of being, it will not learn it. Out of habit, the body will always revert to the previous expression. Even though that position may not be the most optimal, it is the one we know the best. By giving ourselves a chance to experience a new mode of doing over a period of time, we break the tyranny of habit and open up the movement completely.

It was Bruce Fertman, an Alexander Technique teacher, who made me realize that good posture is an attitude, not a static alignment of bones and muscles. During a workshop he taught at my school, he worked with each of us individually. I did not feel as if he were pushing me into position but rather that he was guiding a realignment process that was already happening. When he lay his hands gently along my rib cage while standing in back of me, I felt as if my torso rose out of my pelvic area, like a flower growing upward to be closer to a source of light. I felt no pressure from his hands, only a soft holding.

Those moments that Bruce worked with each one of us were extraordinary. We joked about how each person's face was full of wonder as she felt her body moving under his skillful hands. After working with me, he told me to take a walk around the room. The feeling of lightness and openness continued for a while. I felt taller and needed no effort to stand and walk this way. But I soon noticed that I was beginning to use the muscles in my back to hold the posture. My torso began to feel heavy and to sink down into my pelvic region. I tried to hold the posture and almost immediately felt frozen. I was not experiencing a lightness of being any longer but a state of holding.

It was a gift to be able to witness such a process and to know that effortless movement was indeed possible. It was a door to a whole new way of being.

One day two years later I received a letter from Emily. I had written to invite her to take part in a t'ai chi teacher-training program. "Thank you for your invitation," she began, "but I will not be able to accept it. I have decided to go back to school to become a natural health practitioner. It's something I always wanted to do, but I never thought it possible, with my life being the way it is. But somehow it is possible now."

I like to think that Emily had applied the lesson of taking a giant step to other parts of her life besides t'ai chi. In doing so, she looked at the width and breadth of her life and saw that there was indeed room for something more. She made a decision to no longer subsume her own desires under the needs of others. Emily had put a great deal of time into taking care of her family as well as her invalid mother. Taking a giant step in her life did not necessarily mean that she ignored her responsibilities but that she widened the frame to place herself at the center. Thus her base was no longer the thin tip of the pyramid of other people's claims but the firm wide foundation that came from finding her own center.

I still remember her deep belly laugh and the gleam in her eye when she said to me one day much later, "I can never take a step in the form without hearing your voice saying 'Wider' or feeling the touch of your hand on my foot. First it haunted me. Then I resented it. Then it became my voice. And now it just happens.

"Such a simple thing," she said joyfully, "and yet everything has changed completely!"

13

Not Too Tight, Not Too Loose

Every so often I open the family photo album to look at the picture of me crossing the finish line of the L'eggs Mini Marathon in New York's Central Park in 1980. I do it to motivate myself, now that I have begun cardio-fitness training again.

One day last week I cycled twenty-four kilometers, some of it slightly uphill. I felt good afterward. The next day I cycled twenty kilometers. I arrived home sick to my stomach and bone weary. It said in black and white in my running book: take a day off to recuperate between training when you are beginning, or beginning anew. But I was hungry for the good feeling of the first day, hungry for that spirit of success and top-body performance I had when I crossed the finish line in Central Park in 1980. I sympathize with Fred Lebow's comment in the *New York Road Runners Club Complete Book of Running* (Random House, 1994) that when he heard about someone who ran one marathon a week for a year he thought the guy was crazy—but he also could not help admiring him.

There is no doubt that having a good practice attitude is a question of finding the right balance between intensity, commitment, and time dedicated to training. But what exactly do

I mean by intensity, which is perhaps the most important element in training well? Intensity is a spirit of inquiry that underlies our training style. It can be serious and playful at the same time, but it is not heavy-handed. It penetrates deeply but is not physically painful.

If I were asked to describe someone with a spirit of intensity in her t'ai chi training style, I would automatically think of a student I once had in my class.

From the first evening of the beginner's class, Jenny was always off in a corner practicing while the others were chatting. During class she stood right behind me and followed my instructions to the letter. When the others took a break, she completed what she had been working on before having a cup of tea.

During class Jenny did not talk much. She was not unfriendly, only involved in what she was doing. Soon the others took to calling her "our baby t'ai chi master," and she was teased about it every class. She accepted the joking good-naturedly, but sometimes she bristled a bit. When the class finished the form, most of the students wanted to spend the next semester reviewing. I advised Jenny to join a more advanced class. At the end-of-semester party, the class gave her a ribbon that said: BABY T'AI CHI MASTER. I TRY HARDER!

Her classmates were quite fond of Jenny, but they felt that her training style was a bit extreme. Yet, if asked, they would probably agree that practicing with intensity is necessary to achieve skill in sports or in the arts. Many of them would cheer their children's baseball team and encourage them to strive harder. Others would watch the Olympics and marvel at the capacity of the athletes. Why is it, then, that when someone with such a spirit and commitment to training appears within their own t'ai chi class, these students tease that person for being too intense?

The fact is that people learn t'ai chi for different reasons. If someone is more interested in the social aspects of attending a class, he may find a training spirit such as Jenny's to be inappropriate in a situation he considers more a communal event than anything else. I remember how things were in Taiwan when I trained there in 1986. The master I studied with taught in the park in the early mornings and in his own school in the evenings. There was quite a difference in attitude between the groups of students who attended the two classes. In the morning at least half of the students, many of whom had been coming for years, spent as much time socializing as training. They obviously had a love of t'ai chi and were committed to it, otherwise they would not have come so faithfully or reached the level of skill that they had. But spending time with t'ai chi friends was a central motivation for coming to class.

In the evening classes the atmosphere was completely different. Some of the people who took part in morning classes were also there. But now training was their priority. And train they did, doing push hands for two hours without stopping, or a form class for an hour and a half without even one sip of tea. The teacher was also different. In the mornings he was relaxed and moved at a slow pace. In the evenings there was no question what he expected from his students: effort!

What kind of attitude is appropriate to training? I'm reminded of an analogy that the Buddha used. In talking about the spirit of training, he compared it to the tension necessary for the strings of a musical instrument to produce a pleasant tone. When the string is too loose, the sound is flat. When the tension is too tight, the note is shrill. Not too tight and not too loose. This is the mental and physical state in which optimum training takes place.

Each of us must find the balance that works best for us. That includes choosing to study in a class environment that supports what we want from t'ai chi. One way is not better than another. Just different.

The most important thing is to stay in tune with ourselves.

14

"Thank You for Not Making It Easy"

In *Women Who Run with the Wolves* by Clarissa Pinkola Estés, there is a story about a young woman who is given a small doll by her mother before she dies. The mother tells her daughter, Vasalisa, that whenever she needs help or is unsure, she should heed the advice of the doll. After his wife's death, Vasalisa's father marries another woman, with two daughters, who all proceed to be deep-down mean to Vasalisa. Hoping to get rid of her, the stepmother sends the young woman into the woods to find fire.

Vasalisa is guided in her search by the doll, who always tells her which direction to take. Finally she arrives at the home of a very old and ugly woman. Baba Yaga tells Vasalisa she will give her fire, but only after she performs some chores. She also warns the girl that the tasks must be finished by morning or she will die.

When Vasalisa sees that one of the jobs is to sort out poppy seeds from a huge pile of dirt, she almost faints and says, "Oh, my, how am I going to do that?" The doll whispers that she will take care of it. Vasalisa lies down and goes to sleep.

Sure enough, when she awakes, the task is completed. The story continues with the witch's giving Vasalisa more impossible tasks, each to be completed by morning. The doll accomplishes the task each night while the girl sleeps. On the third morning, Baba Yaga reluctantly gives Vasalisa a fiery skull on a stick and tells her to carry it home. When Vasalisa returns home, her stepmother and half sisters disappear in a puff of smoke. She and her father live happily ever after.

Estes interprets the story as being about qualities that Vasalisa, and indeed all women and men, must develop to grow into fully mature adults. One of the most important, from my point of view, is perseverance. While we all know how important perseverance is, it is a quality that we often sacrifice first when confronted with a seemingly impossible task. Vasalisa, for example, almost faints. While it is understandable that she does so, considering her state of fear, it is a sign that she feels powerless in the face of a difficult task. I don't think there is anyone who has not experienced such despair at least once in his or her life.

The most difficult aspect of any seemingly impossible task is the lack of certainty as to its outcome. We want to know how something will turn out first before we invest any effort. Behind this reasoning there is an assumption that if the outcome does not appear to be favorable, it's not worth the effort even to try. So when we face impossible tasks, there is a built-in program that causes us to give less than we might normally give. This minimizing tendency ensures that the task will not be completed. It is a self-fulfilling prophecy that is remarkably effective in allowing us to undermine our own capability of applying ourselves.

But how does one persevere? The answer is three little words: Just keep going.

Going on, even in the midst of uncertainty, generates an inner strength that comes from not depending on anything and not knowing how things will turn out. It nurtures a trust that whatever situation we meet, we will be able to work with it. While there is no promise that it will turn out in any particular way, the total commitment to the task generates its own state of stability, a state out of which choices, decisions, and action flow effortlessly.

We usually understand this process differently. We think that in order to do something, we need to be motivated. There needs to be a reward at the end, and then the whole effort makes sense. But this attitude creates a kind of dog-seeking-tidbit quality that has us performing like a trained animal. Is the hope of a snack a true source of power or motivation? I think most of us would agree it is not. It's not hard to see that when our motivation is based on such a premise, then when the chips are really down and there is no rescue in sight, we will almost faint, just like Vasalisa.

Experience has taught me that one of the most valuable aspects of learning t'ai chi, indeed of learning anything that requires practice, dedication, and effort, is the positive effect it has on our general attitude to life. In fact, when we take the lessons to heart, then life becomes so much richer. Good moments are part of life, difficult moments are part of life. Both offer us riches. Sometimes the difficult times offer even more opportunities because they ask us to give more than usual. The very effort that is required becomes a source of renewed energy.

It was Sarah who taught me about the reward of committed effort, even in the face of momentous challenge. Sarah had signed up for one of my yearlong intensives, which consisted of eight weekends within a twelve-month period. During this time the group would learn the entire form. When Sarah, a piano teacher, returned for the second weekend, it was clear she was in difficulty: she could hardly remember anything from the previous session. In the second weekend we reviewed elements of the first but then went on to the next section of the form. When Sarah returned for the third weekend, she had only managed to learn some of the moves we had studied in the first weekend.

I knew it would be very difficult for her to learn the form in the weekend intensive series. When I suggested that she would be better served in a weekly course, or by taking private lessons, she rejected my suggestion, mildly but firmly.

"I want to keep trying. I know I'm slower than the others, but I like to think I'm making slow progress. Each time I learn a move, it feels like a gift. I'm okay with things as they are. Are you okay with it?" I answered a hurried yes and we got on with the lesson.

At the end of the year, when the rest of the group had finished the form, Sarah was about a third of the way through it. In the fall she continued with her classmates in the second yearlong, but she attended a weekly class as well. After two years we were able to pop a champagne bottle one night to celebrate Sarah's having finished the form. As we toasted her, the tears flowed down her cheeks. After thanking everyone, she gave a little speech:

"I wanted to give up many times. The thing that kept me going was my thoughts about my own piano students. Many of them want to give up when they reach a difficult point, especially when they don't feel they are making progress. I thought about the things I do and say to help them keep going. This time, though, I said those things to myself. That was a revelation!"

She turned to me and raised her glass, "Thank you for giving me the chance to learn t'ai chi . . . and thank you for not making it easy for me!"

Several years later I found myself finally understanding Sarah's question "Are you okay with it?" At the time I was experiencing what felt like a dead end in my own Zen practice. The initial honeymoon of the first few years of training was over, and I was feeling that all my effort was getting me nowhere. At one point during a retreat an assistant teacher encouraged me to "just keep going."

I burst out in frustration, "That's easy to say. But how do you do it?"

She sat very straight, but the look in her eyes was kind. "Just keep giving . . . that's how you keep going."

I returned to the meditation hall with mixed feelings. A part of me felt that I had already given so much. I had left my family behind to attend the retreat, given up the chance to earn money by teaching a weekend seminar . . . and the list went on. I continued to sit with a kind of I've-given-enough attitude for several more days.

One morning, during the first dawn sitting period, I reached a pitch of frustration. It took all my discipline and years of training to keep me from either screaming in frustration or stamping out, packing my bags, and heading home. At some point I felt as if a spring had sprung within me. I began to cry and continued for several minutes. At the time I didn't think very much, which was unusual for me. The tears just ran down my cheeks, and I continued to sit. I had occupied myself for so long with a forced effort, pushing, wanting more, wanting to get enlightened, wanting it all. It was such a relief to let it all go—for that moment at least.

Suddenly the party to celebrate Sarah's finishing the form,

and the moment she raised her glass to toast, flashed before me. Two things clicked into place. First I recognized that when she had asked me if I could be okay with her slow progress, she was asking me if I could give up my need to see her make it. And then, when she thanked me for not making it easier, she was expressing her gratitude for the opportunity to be able to dwell in each movement, in each moment, rather than my pushing her to go ahead and succeed.

As the sitting period ended, I bowed to the image of her that was still in my mind. I thanked her for her teaching and for her example. I will never forget her.

15

"Tai Chi Ain't Precious"

When I first moved to Germany in 1983, I used to train in a forest near our home. It was an old wood and the trees were very tall. I used to practice near a children's playground in a circle of trees that created a space just large enough for me to do the form. I always felt a special energy the moment I entered the circle.

One day my standing meditation was particularly strong. When I opened my eyes, the bark of the tree in front of me seemed to be covered in symbols. I drew closer, scared and excited at the same time. All sorts of thoughts sped through my mind. I thought I was about to receive a secret, mystical teaching. I spent a long time looking at the signs. Still not knowing what they meant, I returned home with a feeling of having discovered something miraculous.

The next day I returned with my camera. I wanted to photograph the symbols and find someone to interpret them. I was convinced they had special meaning.

I showed the photos to my husband, Norbert, who is a gardener and a landscape architect. He studied them carefully, holding each one for some time. I hung over him in anticipation, bursting to hear what he would say. He turned to me with a slight grin but said seriously, "Where did you take these photos?"

I rushed to explain what had happened. Norbert listened patiently until I had finished. Then he said dryly, "Well, I would say these are photos of the trunk of a tree."

"Yes, that's what they are!" I exclaimed impatiently.

"So?" he asked.

I couldn't believe his denseness. "Don't you see these special symbols?"

He looked again carefully. "No, not really. It looks like tree bark."

I exploded. "You are missing the point!"

"No, you are missing the point, Linda. All tree bark looks like this."

The next morning I rose early and drove to the forest. I hurried to my circle of trees. The marks were still there. I went across the grove to another set of trees. They had similar marks. Either all the trees were trying to tell me something in a secret language or Norbert was right.

After a while I could laugh about the experience. But I also saw how strong my need was to believe in something extraordinary. Those moments in the forest—the quiet beauty of an autumn day, the freshness of new life in spring—were not enough for me. The coolness under the trees in summer, the snow sitting lightly on the branches in winter, were also not special enough for me. I was so busy creating something extraordinary that I missed the uniqueness that was right there.

"T'ai chi ain't precious," Bruce Fertman, an Alexander Technique and t'ai chi teacher, said once to a class of teacher-trainees in my school. I understood him to mean that when we practice the form, we should not be artificially serious or try to be elegant, not try to move like our vision of a t'ai chi master. We shouldn't carry ourselves like a puffed-up courtier bringing something to the queen. That's just another way of not being in our own body but playing in the body of someone else. It is as if we had entered another home and were pretending that we lived there.

When we deeply know that t'ai chi ain't precious, then we can appreciate that every movement and motion is precious. We discover that we do not have to imitate anyone or create something special. That this body of ours is perfect—with all its imperfections. That this body is home.

16
Let the Spirit Master Move You

When I was around six years old, in the middle 1950s, my parents began renting a bungalow for the summer in a camp community about sixty miles from New York. I spent the happiest summers of my childhood there, nestled among people who spoke in thick East European accents, who ate exotic foods like kasha and mushroom-barley soup, and who loved to take children in their arms, hold them close, and stroke any difficulties away with the touch of well-worn hands.

The camp had a strong community feeling. The children were enrolled in a day camp where the principles of team spirit and harmony were emphasized rather than winning or coming out on top. After all, we were the children and grand-children of the former Bolsheviks, communists, socialists, and labor union front-liners who had founded the camp. We learned about gardening, went on walks to mountaintops (where you could see the Empire State Building on a very clear day), or explored the eerie depths of old mines.

Our bungalow was on the outskirts of the camp, so I would have to walk through the woods to reach it. About halfway along the path lay an old house that seemed quietly out of place. It was owned by a couple in their late seventies who spoke in strong German accents and were among the original founders of the camp. Max, who had built the house with his own hands, was to play a crucial role in shaping my young life.

In the evenings everyone congregated in the clubhouse, which had a large central room that served as dining room and dance floor. Two nights a week the tables were cleared away for folk dancing. Our teacher kept us going all evening, and even the small ones among us became masters of flying feet. I still remember the rousing troika number we did and how we sailed under each other's arms in record tempo. We experienced again and again the unity of moving together as if one body, much like a group of people doing the t'ai chi form together.

One night when I was about eight years old, I wandered out to the enclosed terrace of the clubhouse. Men would congregate there and play chess in a fog of pipe smoke. They'd sit in there wearing their caps and jackets even in the middle of summer. During these matches there was collectively at least two thousand years of experience in the room, the youngest person being in his early seventies. Each table was occupied by two men sitting opposite each other, with others standing around them. The seated men were hovering over chessboards filled with dark and light figures that would all of a sudden be moved so swiftly that I could hardly follow. The chess pieces danced in an ancient ritual that was known to everyone except me.

The largest group of men was gathered around a table where Max sat. He was completely different from the way I had known him before. Usually I saw him puttering around the garden, shuffling in his clogs, quietly carrying out his garden chores. But at this table he was the grand master. His eyes followed every move as sharply as a bird of prey tracks its victim. When he moved a chess piece, it was with the swiftness of a seagull skimming the water for fish. In one continuous motion his hand moved from the chess piece to pushing a button on a clock that limited the time of each player's move to sixty seconds. He moved with the finesse of a martial arts master who could flow with grace and yet land a deadly blow with a massive snap!

Max saw me at the edge of the crowd. He studied me for a moment, then a slow smile spread across his face. His eyes glowed as he took a long draw on his pipe. As if reading my mind, he extended his arm toward me and indicated I should come forward. The crowd parted long enough to allow me to be swept in. Max moved over and indicated I should sit next to him. Thus began my initiation into the magical world of the chess wizards.

I spent every evening next to Max. The world of kings and queens, pawns and castles, became my night world. At first nothing made sense, and the moves seemed random, with no meaning. Each night Max explained one figure to me and how it was allowed to move. Each time he began a new game, he would whisper the opening move to me. There were many different openings, some centuries old. A chess master might memorize hundreds of these openings, as well as the play patterns that followed.

One night Max told me it was my turn to play. He sat me on his lap, then whispered an opening move to me. As my young fingers moved toward the piece, Max wrapped his hand around my own. We moved together throughout the game as if we were one. I felt the energy and speed of battle, the lull as the armies regrouped, the cunningness as we faked a retreat, only to advance triumphantly the next second to outflank our opponent. I felt a sense of power emanating from my own center that I knew to be not yet completely mine but something Max was letting flow through me. We played together each evening until the end of the summer.

Suddenly Labor Day weekend, the official end of summer, was upon us. That night there was to be a chess competition, and the winner would be crowned grand master. The event attracted people both from inside the camp and from other communities in the area. The terrace was so packed with men that I had to fight my way through the crowd to get to our table.

Max was waiting for me, along with the glass of orange juice that he always ordered for me. "Drink, drink," he would say. "You have to water your garden," he would say, pointing to my head.

The man sitting opposite Max was unknown to me. He looked at me with surprise as I took my place. His rather stern expression melted for a moment, and I caught the hint of a smile turn the corners of his mouth. He looked at Max and said in a low voice, "So, my old friend, you have found someone after all. That is good."

Max and I opened. The rest of the game was a chess symphony. I don't remember the notes we played, but even now my body remembers the sweeping orchestrations that we soared through. With Max guiding and moving with me, it felt as if I were enveloped in a great wave that continued endlessly across the ocean. At the same moment, Max and I uttered together, "Checkmate!"

Our partner shifted back in his chair. He looked at me with a kindly fierceness. I returned his gaze steadily, confident from our victory and from the presence of Max behind me. I thought he would growl at me in anger, but suddenly he slapped his hand on the table and said exuberantly, "Well done! You've trained her well, my old friend."

As he rose to leave, he leaned over to me and whispered, "Wherever life leads you, little one, remember one thing: Let the spirit of the master move you."

The essence of a living student-teacher relationship is not one of teaching and being taught but one of transmission. The process of transmission implies that something flows between teacher and student. For that to happen, there needs to be a sense of rapport, an open line of communication so that signals can flow unimpeded. We know we've had this kind of precious relationship when even after our teacher has died, his or her spirit still glows in our cells. What our teacher taught us may be important, what he or she imbued in us is vital.

A classical example of this is how dance is taught to young children in many Asian cultures. In Balinese dance, for example, a student begins studying around the age of five. For many months the child does not dance by herself or himself but is moved by the teacher. The teacher wraps himself or herself around the young dancer, and they dance as one. It is as if the space within the teacher's arms were a great womb in which the future dancer was gestating. Not only does the child experience a great deal of security and sense of being cared for, but she directly absorbs the dance into her body through a process of osmosis. Like the baby who sucks nourishment at the breast, the student draws the dance into herself.

There are certain aspects of the teacher-student relationship that can either help the process to flow smoothly or create a dam. This dam can be built through the actions and beliefs on the part of either the teacher or the student—or both. In the Appendix I discuss some aspects of the teacher's role in creating different kinds of training environments. Here I would like to focus on one problematic way in which a student can relate to the teacher.

A frequent way in which we create difficulties for ourselves is to decide, of our own accord, what, when, and how much we are willing to learn. This attitude causes us to pick and choose along the way, rather than start at the beginning and move slowly through the learning stages as they are laid out in whichever particular tradition we are studying. We ignore or criticize what has proved to be a clear path for many people because we think we know what we need. But what we think we need is often only what we want, and when we don't get it pronto, we are out the door.

The challenge is to work skillfully with this attitude so that it will lead to growth and a deepening of our understanding rather than supporting an arrogance that is based on taking oneself a bit too seriously. The little voice of "I know better" or "It should be this way" has detoured more t'ai chi students on the practice road than any other reason I know of.

I am not suggesting that we should leave our minds at the door of the training hall, only our hasty opinions. There may indeed be situations where you decide not to study with a particular teacher or to learn a certain style. What I *am* suggesting is to give yourself, the teacher, and the tradition time to unfold. Things can look very different after several months from the way they appeared during the first class. If the t'ai chi style and the teacher have integrity, then give it a chance to shine. If it doesn't glow for you after a few months, then it's probably time to move on.

Exercises

DRAWING THE T'AI CHI SYMBOL

To prepare to do the exercise, place a photocopy of the accompanying diagrams on the wall. You may recognize this familiar drawing as the so-called yin-yang symbol. The symbol represents the Taoist concept of the state of merging energies of yin and yang in the cosmos, when all things took shape. This state is known as the T'ai Chi, while the formless state from which all things arose is called the Wu Chi (described in the movement Preparation). So for the purpose of this exercise it is appropriate to call this a drawing of the t'ai chi symbol.

The following instructions are meant to help you be precise and to allow the movements to be generated by the turning of the pelvic region. The numbers in the text correspond to those on the diagrams.

Before you begin the exercise, let your eyes roam over the drawing for the left hand, absorbing its image but not studying it intently. Then begin to trace the lines of the symbol with your index finger, beginning at point 1. You may actually touch the paper and later move on to drawing in the air. Do this as many times as necessary until you can draw the symbol without the help of the diagram, or even with your eyes closed.

Begin the exercise by standing with the feet shoulder-width apart and practicing the standing meditation described at the end of Part One. Then do the exercise I Am a Camera from the end of Part Two. As you slowly swivel the hips from

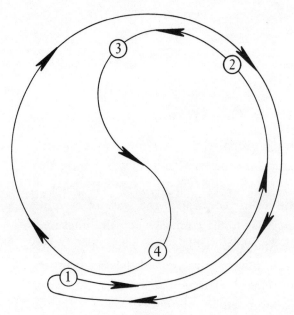

LEFT HAND

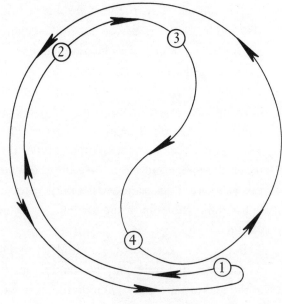

RIGHT HAND

left to right, make sure you are relaxing and sinking in the groin on each side of the body at the end of the swing. The momentum to turn to the other direction comes from sinking and winding up. Be sure not to turn too far or you will strain your back. Keeping your nose in the same vertical line as the navel helps to take care of this problem.

Begin with your right hand at the side of your right thigh. The palm of the hand is almost parallel to the floor, the fingers pointing forward. Turn the waist to the left and begin drawing with your right arm first to the left and then upward to a point corresponding to point 2 on the diagram. You are not touching the paper but drawing in the air in front of it. Let your arm movements be as big as when you would reach up with your arm over your head without standing on your toes.

When your hand is at a position corresponding to point 2, swivel the hips to the right and let your arm follow. When you reach point 3, pivot back to the left and let your arm draw the S downward through the middle of the circle. When you reach point 4, swivel the hips to the right and let the arm draw around in front of your body and then up and all the way around the circle until you reach point 1, where you started. Begin again and draw the t'ai chi symbol seven more times. (If this is too much for you, then try drawing the symbol four times and gradually work up to eight.) Move slowly enough to sense the entire process. Don't move so slowly, however, that you tighten your muscles and impede the flow of movement.

After circling eight times, stand quietly for a few moments. Prepare to begin drawing the t'ai chi symbol with the left hand. If you wish, you may repeat the procedure of first tracing the circle with your finger until you are sure of the movements.

Draw the t'ai chi symbol eight times with the left hand (or four times if that is more comfortable). When you have finished the eight circles, come to a gradual halt. Bring both of your palms in front of your abdomen and stand as if they are holding a volleyball against your stomach. Rest in this position for a few moments, and then slowly move your hands toward your body as if the volleyball is made of a cotton wad. When your hands touch your belly, let them come to rest there with the thumbs over the navel and the index fingers touching. Stand for a few moments with your awareness resting in the center of the triangle created by your fingers and thumbs.

Slide your hands over one another and let them rest on the center of your abdomen. If you wish to end the exercise here, then finish with the massage described on page 33.

Variation 1

It can be very enjoyable to play music during the above exercise. I find flowing, lyrical music the best. If you wish to try doing the exercise with music, first draw the symbol four times to the left and four times to the right without music, being attentive to the execution of the movements as described above.

Once the music begins, it is not necessary to be so strict about how many times you do the exercise in either direction; mix and match between left and right at will. The music encourages freer expression, and it's better not to inhibit the flow by counting.

As the music nears its end, begin to slow down gradually.

End in stillness in the standing meditation, followed by the massage.

One music selection I use often for this exercise is the track "Sahara Moonrise" by Spencer Brewer from the album *Portraits.*

Variation 2

I often encourage my students to move from the stationary form into free movement in the room. Again, it's helpful to use melodic music with rich orchestration.

Begin the exercise in the stationary position. Then begin as in Variation 1. After you have done the movements to the left and right in place, then begin to move around the room. Move in whatever way you wish, letting the music inspire your movements, rather than sticking to the strict form. As you do so, explore the quality of roundness in all your movements—at different speeds and at different levels of height, either by bending the knees or standing up on the toes. Every now and again, return to the stricter form of drawing the t'ai chi symbol, before moving back into improvisation.

Variation 3 (for teachers or group leaders)

If you are leading a group, experiment with not telling the people that they are going to draw the t'ai chi symbol. Guide them as described at the beginning of this exercise. After the exercise is over, ask the group if they recognize a pattern in the movements. Sometimes it takes a while for people to realize that they have been drawing the t'ai chi symbol.

Variation 4 (for groups or group leaders)

Sometimes when a group is standing in stillness at the end of drawing the t'ai chi symbol, I tape a large piece of paper on the wall. I do not tell them they have drawn the symbol so they don't know what is to come. I then invite a student to stand in front of the paper, give her a thick marker pen and tell her to place it on the wall. Then I ask her to continue the exercise she was just doing, keeping the marker on the paper. There's always a few *oohs* and *ahs* when the t'ai chi symbol is drawn for the first time. Everyone gets a chance to draw with the marker, either on a blank paper of their own, or tracing over someone else's drawing.

Variation 5 (for individuals and groups)

Place a sheet of paper on the floor or wherever you can work comfortably. Have a wide selection of colored pens, pencils, or crayons available to choose from. Draw your own t'ai chi symbol in whichever colors you feel attracted to. I encourage you to take time and enjoy the process. After you finish, write down what associations come to mind when you think of yin and yang. Think of aspects of your own life experience and how they could be expressed in terms of these associations

When you are finished, hang your picture on the wall. Using your own diagram, trace the t'ai chi symbol with your finger as described at the beginning of this exercise. You may also wish to stand in front of your symbol and gaze at it, slowly absorbing the impressions, sensations, or thoughts that may arise. In this case I would not use music.

When you have finished, take time to reflect on the associations that have come up for you. Sitting in a meditation posture or writing in a journal may be helpful in deepening the process.

If you are a group leader, bring the participants together at the end of the exercise and let them share their reflections. It should be emphasized that participation is voluntary and that group members may choose whether or not they wish show their picture or talk about it. These periods of sharing can be very rich and allow people to explore the relationship between the symbol, t'ai chi, and their own lives.

The Heart of Practice

The t'ai chi symbol is a type of mandala. A mandala is a visual representation that embodies within its symbols the ideas, beliefs, or stories that have meaning for a person, culture, or spiritual tradition. The creation of the mandala is itself a sacred act. The sand paintings of the Native Americans and the Tibetans are examples of this. Mandalas are documents that bear witness to something sacred but they are not in themselves holy. That is one of the reasons why they are not preserved—afterward they are often either purposely destroyed or allowed to deteriorate.

The history represented in the mandala becomes the present through the efforts of the artist. By doing the exercise of drawing or tracing the t'ai chi symbol, you are enacting an ancient Taoist teaching: All that exists in the universe is in constant flow.

We are the dancing Taoist masters, playing with a t'ai chi ball in a garden as depicted in an old Chinese painting. And we are the children tracing a falling star on a magical night when the heavens are ablaze with light and the universe sacrifices one of its luminous bodies.

Whoosh!

Push

We begin Push by standing in the following position, which is the end of the movement Press: The right foot is pointing straight ahead. The left foot is a full step behind, with the toes pointing outward at an approximate forty-five-degree angle. Seventy percent of the weight is on the right leg. Take care that the right knee is at a ninety-degree angle to the foot and that it is not extending over the toes. If one looked down, the toe should be visible. The left knee is relaxed. Also make sure that you are standing wide enough, which means the inner soles of your feet are shoulder-width apart.

The arms and hands are chest high, at about a forearm's length from the body, and the elbows tend to hang downward. The right palm is facing the body, positioned in the middle of the chest, fingers pointing toward the left. The bottom part of the left hand is pressing against the inside right wrist; the fingers of both hands are moderately rounded.

As you shift the weight backward, separate the hands and draw them back closer to the body to about a hand's width from the chest. The elbows are hanging downward, the palms are facing forward, shoulder-width apart. At this point allow the weight to sink completely on the left leg, and then begin shifting forward, imagining that you are shifting something under the floor as described in Ward-Off.

Shift forward until the weight is about 70 percent on the right leg, relax the groin, and let your weight fall over the forward leg. The pressure on the forward thigh increases considerably, and we feel the right foot being pressed against the floor. Then rock the pelvis slightly forward, and as you do so the arms move slightly forward and upward. We end with the hands shoulder-width apart and not quite an arm's length in front of the body.

There are various ways to think about these last directions, but one way would be to imagine that you are pressing down a spring with your foot. Then at some point the spring releases and the energy flows up through the leg into your arms and extends all the way through to your fingers. At that point if someone or something is standing in front of you and the conditions are right, the person may be sent flying a bit upward and definitely backward.

We must take care with the image of the spring, otherwise the movement will be jerky and piecemeal. In fact the movement is very smooth and asks us to be quiet and deep, penetrating and yet ready to move in a light way.

To see the stance of someone who has executed Push beautifully, look at the picture at the end of Cheng Man-Ch'ing and Robert Smith's book *T'ai Chi: The Supreme Ultimate Exercise for Health.* Professor Cheng has just pushed a young man who is indeed flying upward and backward. The master teacher is standing in perfect alignment, as if he had exerted no effort at all.

DISCOVERING OUR CENTER

Like its name, the movement Push is straightforward. We shift the weight onto the back leg, raise our arms, then shift the weight forward and push. Depending on where we are in our t'ai chi practice, it can look as if we were trying to move a refrigerator or playing catch with a light breeze.

Although Push appears to be relatively simple, it's one of the most difficult t'ai chi movements to do in a relaxed manner. Ideally Push is executed with a minimum of effort and a maximum of natural alignment and optimal use of body power. Yet, the moment we even think about pushing, the body tightens, the chest closes, the eyes narrow, and we raise our hands with tight fingers and have even tighter lips. We think that we "have to push something," but in fact we have to let go of all ideas of pushing.

T'ai chi is often described as the art of effortless power. With Push we begin to see that effortless power does not mean without effort but without any extra or heavy-handed effort. To achieve this, our alignment, the amount of energy used, the timing, and the execution must all flow together seamlessly. Finding that connection can be like having the directions to get to a place but written in a foreign language. There is a great deal of translating and trying out to do before one actually gets to where one wants to go. But it's worth the attempt. When we do sense that connection, it is one of the greatest sources of well-being we can experience in t'ai chi.

Push also lends its name to the partner exercises of t'ai chi known as push hands, or *tui shou*. One of the basic points of push hands is to learn to neutralize the push of someone else and to circulate that energy back so that he will be pushed away through his own power. There are two main styles of push hands: fixed-form and freestyle.

The fixed forms are short sequences in which various movements of the t'ai chi form are strung together to create a push hands form. Students usually begin training in push hands by practicing what is known as "one-hand" push hands, in which a pair joins either their right or left wrists and either pushes or neutralizes a push by turning and deflecting. Once the pair has a feeling for one-hand push hands they can move on to a two-hand form in which both hands and arms are touching in certain positions. A two-hand push hands form can include a set sequence of movements (for example: Ward-Off, Roll Back, Press and Push) from the t'ai chi form. The one-hand and two-hand push hands forms can be practiced either in place, moving within a limited area, such as a circle, or free range.

In freestyle push hands there is no set sequence of moves. One usually begins by doing the one-hand or two-hand partner forms, and then the exercise simply unfolds. It may be stationary, limited to a certain number of steps, or free moving. Freestyle push hands is meant to simply let everything you have learned in t'ai chi flow. It is very exploratory and sometimes confusing, because one has broken away from the fixed forms, which give their own measure of security.

The partner exercises are a wonderful and indeed essential part of learning t'ai chi. Push hands deepens our understanding of the form in unique ways. The things it teaches us about rooting, neutralizing, not meeting force with force, being in our center, and effortless power, as well as giving us a realistic situation in which we can explore the martial applications of the form, make it a very valuable part of t'ai chi training. I would go so far as to say that without participating in some form of push hands exercises, your t'ai chi training, while extremely valuable for health and other reasons, is not really complete.

Many students who begin t'ai chi shy away from partner training because they say they are not interested in the combat or self-defense aspects of the form. There can be many reasons for this, including matters of principle or religious belief, personal experience with violence, and so on. But my experience is that when tui shou is taught in a manner that stresses learning through mutual support, most students are willing to give it a try. When it is presented in this way, then the people standing opposite us are no longer opponents but partners. The issue is not who wins or who loses but how to explore learning together. The goal is not to cause my opponents to lose their balance but for us to help each other to discover our own center.

17
Giving Hands

I was introduced to push hands by one of my first teachers. Although it was more than twenty years ago, I still remember how light his touch was. Pushing freestyle with him was very energetic—and tremendous fun. I had complete faith in him as a teacher. I knew he could push me to my limits—and beyond—but also that he would take care of me so that I would not get hurt.

It was a freeing experience to train in such a safe environment. Because I knew he was pushing with me rather than against me, the boundary between what I allowed myself to do and exploring the unknown melted. There were moments when I felt that "Oh, no!" rising in me, but it would as quickly fade, and the next moves flowed easily. At times it seemed as if we were dancers moving through a grand ballet together.

This teacher taught me what it means to be a real partner. He emphasized that push hands was a learning experience, not a competition. The fundamental ground rule was that what my partner got out of our training together was as important as what I got out of it. From the moment we joined wrists, this was an opportunity for my partner and me to learn something. It was not an excuse for a brawl.

In its deepest expression in push hands, being a partner means that we are committed to helping the person we are working with to explore his or her own fear. It doesn't matter what sport we are training in. Even full-contact boxing, as I was to learn, can be an occasion for exploring fear.

Once I was paired with a very experienced martial arts teacher during one of Master Chen's workshops. In fact, he was a high-ranking tae kwon do instructor. I did not have much boxing experience, but I was willing to give it a try if I could set the terms. I told him I did not want to be punched on the nose or in the chest. I also asked him to use only a small amount of his power because I was afraid he would hurt me. He graciously accepted my restrictions without a trace of hesitation. Even more encouraging, he scrupulously observed the restrictions I had set, never once slipping.

As we continued to box, all sorts of thoughts went through my head. "This is boring for him. He's just being polite. He's just humoring me." I kept searching his face for signs of dissatisfaction, but I couldn't find any. He was paying 100 percent attention to his boxing and to our training together.

As time went on, my feeling of insecurity and inferiority lessened. I began to feel comfortable with what I was doing. Because my partner took me seriously, I took myself seriously. I was no pro, but I could distinguish good punches from bad, and I knew when I was getting stuck in a pattern and needed to shift gears. Our pace increased, though it was still quite comfortable. Occasionally I landed a shot just right, and my partner would smile and say, "Good!"

After fifteen minutes of sparring I felt that I wanted to go beyond the boundaries I had set. I told my partner that I would like to try taking punches in the face, but still not in the chest. Slowly he began to land punches on my face—and on my nose. Once or twice I reacted with surprise, but he waited until I had recovered and was fully present. He asked me each time if I wanted to continue, and, feeling safe, I agreed. By the time we finished, I was taking and giving punches without flinching. I also had a sense of being in my middle and was free of fear. It was one of the most gentle, considerate, and attentive learning encounters I have ever had. And that in a full-contact boxing session!

When I related this story later to others, someone commented, "Well, he's a pro. He's used to giving lessons." Experience has taught me, however, that this kind of consideration and attentiveness is possible at all levels of training. I've trained with people at beginning levels who could extend a caring attitude, and I've trained in teachers' classes where each encounter with a new partner was an ordeal. The level of experience of someone is not the deciding factor in whether or not he can be a true partner. His intention and motivation are the crucial elements.

A story I once heard about basketball star Michael Jordan illustrates the spirit of teamwork and partnership. In the early days of his career, Jordan played as if he were the only player on the court. He would score basket after basket, and the crowd would roar. But the team's coach was not lulled into the star mania of his best player. He knew they could win even more games and points if Jordan would learn to play as part of the team. One day he told his best player that the team was only as good as its weakest player. Jordan immediately understood what the coach was pointing to. From then on, he dedicated his game to assisting others to make baskets—and making baskets himself when that was appropriate. The team went on to be the greatest in history.

Push hands asks us to confront our own greed and impatience, to refuse to join the "I'm only interested in No. 1!" club. It is the art of giving hands, an opportunity to relinquish our need to win or shine so that we can support another person. We both win in the end, because we help to create a training atmosphere in which each of us can feel safe to explore, stretch, and grow. The skill level of everyone will grow in such an atmosphere, as the Jordan story illustrates.

My experience in boxing shows another important aspect of push hands training: It is appropriate and self-nurturing to talk things over, including setting boundaries, with a partner before you begin practicing. It may be as simple as exchanging a few words such as, "I hurt my right shoulder yesterday. I want to go slow today." It may be that you want to train very fast, or do only freestyle, or that you want someone to exert a lot of force so you can practice neutralizing. Or you may want to go slow and only do fixed-form push hands.

If you have had negative experiences with push hands, or you do not feel safe in a training situation, it is best to bring this up with your teacher and partner. But it is a fact of life that not every teacher or training partner will be receptive to your request. Some teachers and students feel that the way to overcome one's fears is by staying in the situation and working with it the way it is. Some teachers may see such requests as a challenge to their authority or as a sign of audacity, as if you think you know better than they do what is good for you. And some teachers and partners simply aren't bothered by what may be bothering you, and whether they try to or not, they don't see it as an issue.

That doesn't mean that you should continue training in a situation when you are uncomfortable. There are teachers and training partners who will be receptive to your suggestions or requests. I encourage you to look for a push hands training situation where you feel safe. There are several ways to do this.

If push hands is not offered by your teacher, or not in a way you wish to train, you may be able to find a few other classmates who are interested in practicing outside class. At the end of this part there are preliminary exercises, especially Leading and Following, that can be practiced over and over. These exercises are a good place to start to develop some of the basic skills used in push hands training. Books about push hands practice, though not a substitute for quality instruction, may at least be a place to start. There are also t'ai chi meetings on a national (such as A Taste of China, which usually occurs in Virginia around July Fourth weekend) and on a local level in which push hands training is offered. Consult the various publications, including *T'ai Chi* magazine, in which these events may be advertised. The internet is also a valuable resource in this respect.

I have seen so many students move from refusing to do any push hands to enjoying practice, once they found the right training environment for themselves. Keep looking! It's worth the effort.

18

The Masters of Ting

Some of the most famous push hands bouts in t'ai chi folk-lore, if not history, were actually nonevents. The story usually goes something like this: Two great masters are scheduled to meet in public for a push hands competition. This in itself is a sensation, because most matches take place in private. So hundreds of spectators filling a crowded hall eagerly await the masters' arrival. When the time comes, the old men (they're always old and always men) enter the arena and step onto the platform. They bow to each other and spend a few moments in preparation. Then they face each other and join wrists, the classic beginning posture of push hands.

For several minutes nothing happens. Many people are sitting on the edge of their seats. Suddenly the two masters take a step back, bow to each other, and leave the ring. The match is over.

The audience breaks out in excited chatter. Every moment of the "bout" is discussed in detail. The crowd is animated and totally involved in the "action." It is only natural for us to ask, What in the world are they so excited about?

Such stories are part of the mythic tales of t'ai chi. And

like all myths, they encode values, principles, and statements about the subject they portray. In this case the key aspect is to delve into why the meeting between these two masters was considered a great match. What is this much ado about nothing?

The audience of t'ai chi aficionados was, of course, initiated into the subtleties of what was going on. Rather than feeling cheated of action, they felt they had been honored with the most subtle expression of push hands mastery. The two men were masters of *ting*, the quality of listening, whose cultivation is at the center of push hands training. The spectators knew that such an experience is rare; to be in its presence is a great gift.

Ting, sometimes translated as "listening energy," can be described as an open receptiveness, a dynamic sensing both of my own and of my partner's state of being. When we lay our wrists against each other in the opening movement of push hands, we are "listening" to each other.

Each master was waiting for a lapse in the attention of the other, waiting for a moment when the flow of present-moment awareness was broken. If either of the masters had lost this awareness, the other would have sensed it immediately. Then he would have responded instantly and pushed the other person out.

Ting is present in every moment of push hands, whether one is standing still in the opening posture or moving energetically. Ting is a very light quality, not to be confused with a lack of intensity. It is light but pierces to the center. That is why it cannot be present when t'ai chi partners are playing with brute force or a stark intent to win.

Ting is not something reserved for push hands. The quality of listening with our hands is essential to many healing arts, like shiatsu or Reiki. It is at the heart of loving relation-ships, and it is the essence of a potter's mental state as he sits and shapes a masterpiece on a wheel. When we listen in a way that expresses unimpeded ting, then the action flowing from this is a response, not a reaction. A response implies that there is no separation; when we react, there is a gap. Response flows, reaction confronts. Response is a leaf being carried down a stream; reaction is when it gets wedged be-tween the rocks.

There are many things that can block the capacity to listen in push hands. At the center of all of them is fear. We can be afraid of anything: getting hurt, losing face, intimacy. In all these cases, push hands feels like an examination, and there is a focus on the result. But ting is about process, and process is about moment-to-moment awareness. We can be more aware or less aware, but we cannot fail. Even if we are very distracted, the moment we notice we have drifted away is also a moment of awareness. In push hands, the moments of drifting away are usually when we get pushed.

I once received a very poignant teaching from another true master of ting. In 1986 I had the good fortune to study t'ai chi for six weeks in Taiwan with a t'ai chi master known for his amazingly soft but effective style of push hands. The first morning I joined his class I stood to the side when the push hands training began. Since I was new, I waited to be invited to push. But the teacher's students were very kind and included me in the activity immediately.

I stood facing a man about my own age. We greeted each other and then took up the beginning push hands stance. I waited. And waited. Nothing happened. My mind began working fast, trying to figure out what my partner was doing.

Over and over again the question came up, "What is he wait-ing for?"

Eventually I decided to get things moving. I began to push ever so slightly. I could feel nothing, and so I began pushing with a bit more power. Again I felt nothing, or almost noth-ing, so I increased my push. Suddenly my partner turned at the waist and I headed straight for the wall. Another man got between me and the wall and served as a cushion. The only thing that suffered a blow was my pride.

My partner was laughing happily and came over to shake my hand. I was miffed, to say the least, and I wanted to tell him what he could do with his hand! But I tried my best to conceal my hurt feelings and accepted his invitation to push again.

This time I was not going to get caught. I would stand until the end of time if necessary, but I was not going to push first. The only thing I didn't reckon on was that my partner had much stronger legs and endurance than I did. At some point, just about the time my legs were going to give way, I shifted my weight backward ever so slightly. Suddenly I was flying through the air, only to land in the arms of another student who had, apparently, been standing behind me the whole time. When I saw that he had prevented me from fall-ing off the terrace where we were practicing, my irritation turned into heartfelt gratitude. I thanked him warmly.

At this point the teacher intervened. He approached me and raised his arm, a sign that he wanted to push with me. I placed my wrist against his and felt as if I was leaning my hand against a cloud. We slowly did the two-hand push hands exercise, the teacher allowing me to get some sense of bal-ance and flow of movement again. At some point I felt a tiny spark of competitiveness rise in me. If I could push him, maybe I could get some respect from this bunch.

Just as the master was on his back leg, that spark burst into flame. I pushed ever so slightly—and again I was hurtling into someone's arms. "You want too much to win," the teacher said. "But when you want too much, you cannot listen. And then it is easy to push you."

I never forgot his lesson. It wasn't that I suddenly could do what he asked me to do. But push hands took on another meaning for me. I learned that to cultivate ting was not only to try to be awake and aware in the present moment but to listen to my own heart, no matter what it was saying. Push hands became an opportunity both to train with others and to tune in to myself. When I practiced push hands in this way, there was tremendous space. Sometimes it was filled with my need to do well, sometimes I could just be present for what was happening. Whatever was going on, it was boundless.

19
Only Don't Know

One night when I pushed with Tony, I noticed that most of the time she was either grabbing my arms or frantically pulling her own away from me. When I mentioned this to her, she became defensive. By way of explanation, she said, "Well, I don't know what I am doing." I realized later that she was pointing to something that many people share when doing push hands: an insecurity about not knowing what to do. And because of its unpredictability, many people shy away from practicing the partner exercises of t'ai chi.

A fear of not knowing is really a fear of not being in control. And that's often the first thing that comes up when we stand opposite someone and begin push hands. We don't know if the other person is better than we, we don't know what will happen in the next moment, how we will be pushed, or whether we will even feel the movement before it happens.

The secret of push hands is to know that not-knowing is exactly the state of mind we wish to cultivate. When you just don't know, then you're present in every moment. You're not attached to what came before and you don't project into the future. Defending our sense of pride, struggling to maintain our balance, or trying to outmaneuver our partner are all examples of not being in the present moment. In such a state, everything gravitates toward winning, protecting oneself, or not losing face. It also takes a great deal of energy and leaves one exhausted when we push in this way. Trying to maintain control is like trying to determine where a snowflake will fall.

What is don't-know mind and how does it manifest in push hands? Don't-know mind is beyond technique. It is a state of complete openness and readiness. There is no premeditation or planning or projecting. When someone pushes us, we respond with the lightness of a feather dancing in the wind.

There is a moment in the film *Forrest Gump* that beautifully portrays this state of responsiveness. In the opening titles, a feather is blown about by the wind. Repeated bursts cause the feather to dance magically throughout the opening scene. Even without knowing what the movie is about, you have a sense it will be about the twists and turns that we experience in life.

The film documents the story of a simple man named Forrest Gump. He is trusting and believing, never rebels, simply tries to do his best. Like the feather, he is blown about by life's events. We watch his story unfold over three decades, from the 1960s to the 1990s, reliving the sweep of the hippie era, the Vietnam War, Watergate, space exploration, the fall of the Berlin Wall, and finally the yuppie nineties. A favorite expression of his mother's was that life was like a box of candy and that you could never know what you'd find when you unwrapped a piece.

Every moment of push hands is a piece of candy waiting to be unwrapped. When we can really experience it this way, then we can be open to all the surprises and opportunities it has to offer. We can delight in the cherry center, even if we were hoping for caramel. This is a simple but delicious way of talking about don't-know mind.

Another example of don't-know mind was beautifully portrayed in a TV documentary on the world's leading woman free climber. She described in the most minute detail how her hands sensed the right crevice to use when climbing. The camera followed her as she moved across a huge face of rock as swiftly and as effortlessly as a spider. Each time she reached for a new crevice or hold, it was a movement filled with grace and sensuality, no matter how fast she was progressing. She did not think about the movements but relied on her intuition. Although she did not actually say that she became one with the rock face, that was how it seemed.

There is a similar process going on in push hands: The moment we find ourselves thinking about what is going on, the flow stops. And when the flow stops, that's often the moment when we get pushed out. Something has intervened that has broken the seamlessness of the encounter. Once the seam is broken, then there are lots of jagged edges that our partner can use as a handle to upset our balance and push us out.

I once saw someone wearing a T-shirt inscribed with one of the favorite expressions of Korean Zen master Seung Sahn. Blazoned across this young man's chest was a phrase that sums up the experience in each moment of push hands: ONLY DON'T KNOW!

Exercises

Back-to-Back

I often do preliminary exercises before push hands training to set the stage for a more relaxed training atmosphere. One of these exercises is called Back-to-Back.

Begin by finding a partner who is approximately the same size as you. Sit back-to-back on the floor. (It is also possible to sit on stools.) You may sit either cross-legged or with your legs stretched out in front of you, whichever is more comfortable. Let your backs be as much in contact as possible.

Take a few moments to sense the impressions that arise. Just register them; try not to analyze them or get lost in their meaning.

Then imagine that you have an itch in your back. Your partner's back is a friendly tree or surface that you can rub your back against to relieve the itchiness. Take time to enjoy this part of the exercise. It often creates a lot of giggles and playfulness.

When you are ready, hook your elbows with your partner's and then begin to move slowly back and forth, or in circles. Neither person is leading or following, just sensing. Try to maintain contact in as many places on the back as possible. If you find you are sliding apart, adjust yourselves so you are close again.

Continue at a slow pace. Allow yourself to be carried by the movement. Some students begin to lean their heads against their partner's back and let the movements lull them into a deep relaxation.

There is no specified amount of time the exercise should last. If you are leading a group, be attentive to each person's experience. Try to end the exercise at what feels like a natural point. I have done it for as long as thirty minutes and as short as ten.

When it feels right to end, come to a slow stop and remain sitting back-to-back with your eyes closed.

Take time to again feel into your back. After a few moments ask yourself, "Where does my back end and where does the back of my partner begin?" Feel the answer rather than saying it out loud.

When you have taken some time to be with this question, prepare yourself mentally for the exercise to end. Slowly separate from your partner. After a few moments, turn around and face him or her. Take some time to share your experiences.

People often report afterward that it was impossible to feel the boundary of their own skin. Only when they physically separated from their partner could they feel their own back again. This realization can have a profound impact on a person's sense of connection to other people. Realizing that the so-called boundaries between us are an illusion can open up different avenues of thought or discussion. In fact this exercise can be used in many different settings, from the classroom to the meditation hall.

Its effect in a push hands context is that when those pairs who have been sitting back-to-back stand up to do push hands front-to-front, there is a much different quality in the way they work together compared with before. It is softer and more gentle.

Ting: The Quality of Listening

This exercise is a meditation on being: your own and your partner's. You will be tuning in to yourself and your partner on the level of sensation. The directions ask you to become aware. It is important to "listen" to whatever you feel without overlaying it with judgments or the wish to change things. If you sense tension in your back, for example, then just note "tension." Name the sensation for what it is and then let it go.

Stand about an arm's length from your partner. Take a moment to exchange hellos or names if you don't know one another. If you wish to be more formal, then bow to each other.

Close your eyes. (You may also keep your eyes open, however, if that feels more comfortable. In that case, just look straight ahead with a soft gaze.)

Become aware of your own body as you stand. Feel your connection to the earth through your feet. Let your attention move from the feet upward through the body, taking a moment to rest in the lower legs, upper legs, pelvis, back, chest, neck, and head. Allow yourself to linger in each body area and to sense as much as possible. It can take some time to become aware, and to begin with it may be very subtle and not register so clearly. It may help to imagine that as you breathe, the body part where your awareness rests fills with the breath. In any case, don't force anything. With repeated practice and patience, you will become more familiar with the process and begin to map your own understanding of what is going on within you.

When you have sensed your head, then become aware of your own body as a totality. Stand for some moments with this sense of the whole body. Then begin to expand your awareness beyond yourself. Let it expand at its own pace, without forcing it. Gradually you will become aware of the person standing in front of you. Just be aware of whatever you seem to be sensing.

After a few minutes, open your eyes. You and your partner should step forward into the traditional one-hand push hands stance (the left foot is forward and parallel to your partner's forward foot; the right foot is turned forty-five degrees outward). Raise your right wrist and touch the right wrist of your partner. Stand for some moments just registering the sensations that flow into you.

You may also find it helpful to ask yourself certain questions to help you tune in. Don't try to ask all the suggested questions, but pick one or two that are most relevant to you in this situation. For example, ask yourself:

"How heavy is my partner's touch?"

"Can I sense any other part of his body besides his wrist?"

"Can I feel my own contact to the floor?"

"How heavy is my own touch? Are my biceps tense?"

"Where is my partner placing his weight?"

"Do I feel a pushing energy, even though nothing is happening?"

"Am I leaning forward or drawing back from my partner?"

A comfortable amount of time for this part of the exercise is about two to four minutes. End the exercise by slowly releasing your wrists. Return to the standing posture facing each other. Close your eyes and tune in to your body again. Ask yourself, "Has anything changed since I began the exercise?"

Open your eyes and sit down with your partner for a chat. Let your partner begin by saying what he sensed about you.

When your partner has finished, then share what you experienced about yourself. Then switch roles.

Sharing in this way allows for the pair to get to know one another, which is always helpful for partner work. Also, each person has a chance to check his or her own perceptions against the perceptions of the partner. As often as the responses are similar they are different. And that makes for some very interesting learning opportunities.

The Empty Mirror: Leading and Following

The empty mirror is a powerful image for the kind of attitude that is helpful in push hands training. A mirror is empty because it simply reflects back whatever stands in front of it. It doesn't form opinions, judge, become afraid, or want to win. There is no ego that gets in the way of mirroring back the image. In these exercises of leading and following, we want to be like the empty mirror. Someone leads, someone follows. Just that.

It is helpful in partner exercises like these for the students to have clear roles. In the case of the following exercises, except variations 4 and 7, the role is to be either the leader or the follower. For the sake of clarity, in all the exercises, partner A is the leader and partner B is the follower.

The beginning and end of each variation are very important. Always begin by greeting each other in some form. Exchange hellos, bows, or names, or simply look at each other with kind eyes. Then agree on which person has what role: leader or follower. Take your positions and then stand together in silence for a few moments before beginning.

The most important aspect of these exercises is to take your time. Begin slowly and build slowly. Rather than rush through the various exercises, take the time to get the most out of them. Each of these exercises is a very deep learning process in itself. They can also be a lot of fun.

Variation 1: Mirroring in Place

Partners A and B stand opposite each other with their feet parallel and shoulder-width apart.

A begins by lifting his right arm and moving it slowly through the air. B follows with her left arm. A should make large movements and do them slowly enough so that B can stay with him quite easily.

After a few minutes, A switches to the left arm and B follows with her right arm. To begin with, just move one arm or the other. This gives B time to train in the art of following.

Gradually increase the speed until you are both moving faster but still together. The movements can also be smaller as time goes on. Remain in place throughout the exercise.

A slows down gradually and then stops. A and B stand opposite each other for some moments in stillness. Then A and B switch roles.

Variation 2: Mirroring the Whole Body in Place

This exercise can follow the first one or be done in the next lesson. Begin the same way as in variation 1. After moving one arm and then the other, A should then begin moving both arms, still remaining in place. After B seems to be following well, A should also begin incorporating movements with his legs, raising and lowering, circling in the air, and so forth. Remain in place.

A can also add movements such as raising and lowering the shoulders, turning at the waist, moving the head, shaking the whole body, kicking. As A changes from one kind of movement to another, he should make sure that B is following the change. If not, he should pick B up where she is and then continue. After a time, A and B switch roles.

Variation 3: Mirroring in Space

In this exercise, the pair will begin to move in the room. They begin as in variation 2. When A has moved both arms, then he begins to take steps. A moves slowly and in a pattern that is easy to follow. One step left, one step right, and so on. As time goes on, A moves faster and in different ways: taking big steps, tiny steps, running, jumping, turning round and round, on tiptoe, on the heels, A adds arm movements, increasing both the speed and the complexity as time goes on. As the exercise draws to an end, A slows down gradually until he comes to a stop. The pair should rest in stillness for a few moments before switching roles and beginning again.

Variation 4: No Leader, No Follower—In Place

Begin by standing opposite each other in stillness for some time. Then one person begins to move. This just seems to happen naturally without being decided upon beforehand. As soon as one person moves, the other follows. The follower may continue to follow as long as she wishes. At some point during the movement, the follower should take over the lead. Let the transitions be slow and deliberate to begin with, but with no verbal exchange. As the speed increases, see if the change from leader to follower can flow as smoothly as possible.

This is not a particularly easy exercise because it asks us to be able to become the leader or the follower in a moment. It asks us to be completely present in our role and then drop it in the next moment. How the exercise will be experienced depends a lot on the chemistry of the pair working together. But no matter what, it is a profound exercise in giving and receiving, and ultimately in letting go.

Variation 5: Connecting at the Wrists

Begin by standing opposite each other as usual. Each person should then place his or her right foot forward so both feet are parallel to each other. The left foot of each person should be one step behind and pointing outward at a forty-five-degree angle.

A and B place their wrists together. During the whole exercise, the wrists should always be touching at some point.

For the beginning of the exercise, A and B stand in place. A is the leader and moves his arm in various ways, making circles, going up and down, left and right. A gradually increases the speed of the movements until he is going quite fast.

To end, the pair slows down gradually and then stops and stands quietly. Then A and B switch roles and repeat the exercise.

Variation 6: Connected and Moving in Space

This exercise is the same as variation 5, except that A and B will begin to move around the room. It is important first to practice in place as in variation 5 and then to begin to move slowly. A should make sure that B can follow his steps and stay connected at the wrist. As the exercise continues, A can increase the speed, varying the size of the movements and steps as described in variation 3. No matter what happens, the focus is on staying connected at the wrists.

Variation 7: No Leader, No Follower—Moving in Space
Begin as in variation 6. But now there is no one leading or
following. One person can initiate the movement, but then
the exercise simply develops. Go on for as long as is comfortable. Come to a gradual stop and stand in stillness before
ending the exercise.

The Heart of Practice
Push hands is an opportunity to reach across the barriers we
set up between each other and to realize our common humanity. Having a sense of being one with our partner con-
firms that push hands is not about training in the ways of war,
but in the way of peace.

Exercises like Back-to-Back, Ting, and the Empty Mirror
can be a step toward healing the separation that exists between us, a separation created by fear. Vipassana meditation
teacher Sharon Salzberg speaks eloquently in her book *Lovingkindness: The Revolutionary Art of Happiness* on how crossing
the boundaries that separate us is stepping into the zone of
peace:

> The legacy of separation impoverishes the spirit. Seeking
> only to protect ourselves, we cannot genuinely connect
> with others, we cannot see what needs our love, and we
> struggle with terrible aloneness. In trying to reach others
> from the stance of our isolation, we are like weary travel-
> ers preparing for a dangerous border crossing, cautiously
> hoping to reach a new land and make contact, secretly
> believing it will not be possible. Veering between fitful
> hope and underlying insecurity, we have no peace. Imag-
> ine the relief of discovering that there is no such border
> to be crossed. It is only through seeing our fundamental

connection with the world that a life of true peace becomes possible.[1]

The exercises on leading and following also have much to teach us. We learn a great deal about ourselves in our handling of the two roles. Some people have difficulty leading, some have difficulty following. Sometimes we notice this ourselves, but often it takes the reaction of another person to show us what we are doing.

Give these exercises your kind and open attention. At the point where our wrists or backs meet there is an opportunity for intimacy and sharing that unites us at the most basic level of our humanity. It is deep listening in a most compassionate and open way.

Get the Needle at the
Sea Bottom

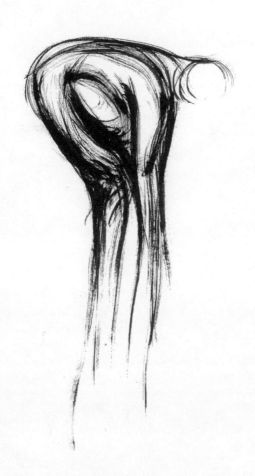

I have always wondered what the name of this movement, Get the Needle at the Sea Bottom, refers to. Perhaps it is a reference to a story from Asian folklore. Maybe it's the Chinese way of saying "find a needle in a haystack." The name makes me think of a social healing ritual practiced by Arctic shamans, when during a trance they would travel to the bottom of the ocean to ask the Princess of the Sea to restore the once bountiful hunting to their communities.

Get the Needle follows the movement called Step Up, Deflect, Intercept, and Punch. The difference between the names, one poetic and full of imagery, the other cut and dry and focusing on the martial arts application, illustrates so well the polar aspects of t'ai chi. In fact, both elements are important in doing the form. The poetic imagery suggests a lightness and sense of artistry to the movements; the functional helps to underline that they are also precise and effective.

Begin the movement by standing with the left foot one step ahead of the right and pointing straight ahead. The right foot is positioned at a forty-five-degree angle to the right. The right hand is extended forward in a vertical, lightly closed fist at waist level. The left hand is at the side of the left thigh in what is called a "sitting palm" position so that it is in line with the thigh and the palm faces down.

Step up completely onto the left foot (without leaning too far forward) so that the right foot comes away from the floor. At the same time the right fist goes slightly forward. Then set the right foot down where it was before and shift the weight completely backward onto it. As you shift backward, open the right fist and pull the right hand slowly toward the breast, the fingers pointing downward, and lightly place the index and middle finger of the left hand on the inner right wrist. As you draw the fingers back, pull the left foot back so that it comes to rest on the toes just to the side of the right foot.

Now bend downward until the fingers of the right hand are almost touching the floor. Be careful to go only as low as is comfortable without straining your back and without straightening the knees. When in doubt, only bend slightly. (If you have back problems, including but not limited to a history of slipped disks, lower back pain, etc., do not bend down at all, or only do so under qualified medical supervision. Simply proceed to the next movement.)

Begin to roll upward (vertebra by vertebra) until you are standing upright. Most of the weight is on the right foot, which is solidly planted. The left foot is delicately waiting with the heel raised and weight balanced between the toes and the ball of the foot.

Get the Needle at the Sea Bottom is one of the movements described in this book with a particularly effective martial arts application. We reach forward to grab the hand of our opponent and then as we go downward we drag him to the floor. If we would bring our hands up rapidly, we could strike him under the chin or in the throat. The movement could also be used to strike someone who was already on the floor. Well-coordinated attacks to the eyes, solar plexus, and so on could be quite disabling, if not fatal.

It is very helpful to know the martial applications of the t'ai chi movements because they help us to perform them with precision. Some of my students are not comfortable with martial images, however, and so I always suggest alternatives. For example, Get the Needle at the Sea Bottom reminds me of the elegant gesture of a Renaissance courtier who might bend down in this way to retrieve a handkerchief. Or you might think of it as reaching down to pierce an apple with a sharp stick. Whatever works for you is fine, as long as it clarifies your sense of what you are doing and gives life to the movement.

20

The Treasure

When people practice together, I often find one person looking wistfully at the others. Early on in my teaching career, I wondered what was going on. When I would ask a student if something was bothering him, he would usually give an explanation such as, "Oh, she does that movement different from how I do it. I was just wondering which way was correct." I was taken in by this explanation and would cheerfully go on to discuss the technical details of the move. Sometimes we would spend the rest of the class happily trying out various permutations. These classes were usually the most animated and fun, with everyone leaving with the feeling that some good hard work had been done.

Then one day I was looking at a photo of myself at an international t'ai chi meeting. The photo was taken as I was watching some colleagues do a push hands form. I had the same wistful expression on my face I had seen so many times on the faces of my students. Suddenly I realized what was really going on.

My own wistful expression had nothing to do with whether the people I was watching were doing a movement different from how I did it. The fact was, I was feeling that they were much better at push hands then I was. At the moment the shutter snapped, I was wondering if I could ever be as good as they were. My look showed not only that I was busy uncovering their treasure but that I was burying my own at the same time.

One of the surest ways to destroy our pleasure in learning t'ai chi is to compare ourselves with others. In truth, though, I don't know anyone who doesn't sometimes get caught in this trap. To compare ourselves with others—and mostly to come up short in the competition—is such a part of our upbringing that we tend not to notice it anymore. We have even invented the euphemism "constructive criticism" to explain the way we "support" each other. If we look carefully, even so-called constructive criticism always begins from the position that something is wrong.

There is nothing harmful in acknowledging that someone may be more skilled than we are. When we do so in a way that is not denigrating to ourselves, we can open ourselves to learning in a positive and supportive way. It takes real awareness, however, to stay open, because the feeling of not being good enough is so ingrained it's almost easier for us to deal with. It is a sad but true fact that we are often more comfortable with self-criticism than with realistic assessment of our talents. It is easier to see someone else's qualities than to appreciate our own.

A story I was told as a child illustrates this point well. I often tell it to my beginning students:

There was once an elderly man who lived in poor circumstances in a remote village. One night he has a dream in which a figure tells him there is a treasure to be found at the foot of a castle drawbridge located in a city several days' journey away. Upon awakening, he sets out on a long, arduous trip to the city.

When he finally arrives, he meets a captain at the draw-bridge. After hearing about the man's dream, the captain tells him that he also dreamt the night before, but in his dream a man discovers a precious treasure under the stove in his own house. The old man hurries home, digs up the treasure, and dedicates his life to prayer and to helping the destitute.

Like this man, we are often busy looking for a treasure under other people's stoves rather than appreciating the one that sits under our own. This is as true in learning t'ai chi as in anything else.

My students once gave me an important lesson in uncovering the treasure that is at the heart of each of our own forms. We were at the end of the first year of an intensive t'ai chi course, and they had just finished learning the form. Someone had brought a video camera to class. I had the bright idea to film each person doing the form and to look at the videos later that weekend.

We filmed the students in groups of three to cut the shooting time. Almost everyone had stage fright, and there were lots of shy glances and efforts to straighten clothes and arrange one's hair. As I watched their faces while they were being filmed, I could see that most of them had rather somber expressions. Their lips were tightly drawn, their movements rather stiff. Obviously all were quite nervous.

I had a secret motivation for filming them, which I did not reveal to anyone. I hoped that as a result of seeing themselves—and especially noticing their mistakes—it would give the class extra motivation to practice through the long summer break. I calculated that they would all judge themselves critically and vow to eliminate their mistakes. My "constructive criticism" motor was in high gear.

Late Sunday afternoon arrived and we prepared to watch the video. There were lots of nervous giggles and coughs as I set up the video recorder. The class made themselves comfortable with cushions and beverages. It all had the atmosphere of waiting for the main feature to start.

As the video began to play, all eyes focused intensively on the screen. As the first students recognized themselves, two groaned and the other said under her breath, "Oh, no, why did we have to be first?" It continued like that until the very last pair finished the form.

As I shut off the video I turned to the group. I was ready for serious discussion, for each student to take notes of what he or she needed to work on. I was not prepared for the sea of starry-eyed men and women who stared back at me. I sensed that things were not going as I thought they would, but I still hadn't twigged to what was really going on.

"Well," I began, trying to get the group to focus. "What do you think?"

No reaction. I decided that perhaps they were so flattened they needed some time to find words again. So we just sat for a while in silence.

Slowly the group came to life. Susan was the first one to speak.

"I was worried about making a fool of myself, and then on top of that to have it recorded on video." She paused. "But you know, I'm really surprised. I think I look okay."

John spoke up next. "I kept looking for some drastic mistake. Because everyone is always talking about my posture, I kept looking for the parts where you all say I am crooked. But it's not so bad, is it?" He paused and then added, "You know, it's pretty good." The rest of the class spoke up in much the same vein.

I was shocked. My plan, as far as I was concerned, had completely backfired. Instead of seeing how many mistakes they had made, the students were busy praising themselves and each other. At this rate they wouldn't practice at all. I vowed never, ever to do this video exercise again.

And then I looked at their beaming faces. They all stood up to stretch their legs, and I noticed they carried themselves taller and more erect. Then they began some animated discussions. Four of them eagerly debated whether a move should be done Marianne's way . . . or maybe Sharon's way was closer to the t'ai chi principles. Joseph realized he had been making too much effort in doing the move Push, whereas Bill saw for the first time why he was having difficulty with the move Crane Spreads Its Wings. Their cheerful, loud, and detailed discussion lasted for more than half an hour. I just sat and watched, kept my mouth shut, and let the lesson of it all sink in.

And there was a big lesson for me to learn that day. It was the lesson of the old man and his search for treasure. I was very much like the old man of the first part of the story: I wanted my students to look somewhere else besides in themselves for the treasure.

And my students were more like the old man of the second part of the story. They discovered that they didn't need to search somewhere else for the treasure. They just needed to uncover the one that was in each of them.

That is the feeling we should cherish each time we do the form. That is the treasure at the heart of our t'ai chi form.

21

"The Secret Is to Practice"

Everyone who practices t'ai chi will experience moments of stuckness. It happens in every class I teach. Someone will learn a move, then get stuck later and say, "I can't remember the move." Usually it's more a case that we have convinced ourselves that we can't remember the move. Our own thoughts block us, trapping us in self-doubt. The body, which feels somewhat at home with the move, might be able to find the way if our thoughts would not detour us. At that moment we can sense a deep loneliness.

I remember how painful it was for me when I kept forgetting the end of the sword form. I had been attending a twelve-week course and could not make it to the last class. Later, someone showed me the moves I had missed, which also happened to be the end of the form. I felt confident I had learned everything and didn't give it another thought.

As I practiced the next day, everything went fine until I reached the last section. I came to an abrupt halt in the form, my arm holding the sword in midair. I simply couldn't remember what came next. The more I tried to remember, the more I came up empty. I returned to an earlier section and tried to find the connection but always hit the same snag. I finally asked a classmate to show me the moves again. I had to work very hard with this part of the sword form. No matter how many times I practiced, it never felt right. Whenever I reached the last section, I faltered. I did all sorts of mental gymnastics to remember, including repeating key words to jog my memory. Nevertheless, the end of the form always felt choppy.

One day as I practiced and was about to reach the point where I always stumbled, I noticed something. First, I sensed how tense I was. And then I caught a thought racing through my mind: "You're not going to make it!" Just after that I got stuck again.

Suddenly I realized what was happening. Deep inside me was a voice that programmed my own failure. That voice expressed an attitude that was so overpowering that the only relief was to fail. Then I felt like a failure. The vicious cycle was complete.

Not being able to remember the next move is not a sign of failure. The simple fact is that we have forgotten the move. We have a small problem. And yet it can feel immense because we have an emotional investment in the situation: it seems that our very sense of self-worth is at stake. We can be so overwhelmed and pained by this self-judgment that we never really investigate what is going on. The sense of being a failure duplicates itself, dupes us, and continues its merciless course.

One way to break the grip of this assumption is to prove that it is simply untrue. When a student forgets a move and seems to be stuck in a paralyzing self-judgment mode, I do the following guided meditation with him:

We begin the form and I ask him to be aware of his body

moving in space. When we reach the move where he is stuck, I ask him to stand quietly. Then I continue:

"Gently turn your attention to your breathing. Feel the air flow in and out. If you notice that you are pushing or thinking about the next move, just let that go. . . . There is nothing that you have to achieve. Just trust this moment of quietness and let go into it. . . .

"When you are ready, turn your attention lightly to your position at this moment. Try to feel the next movement taking shape. Let it express itself any way it wishes. Don't force it. There is no right or wrong."

After some time of quiet standing, I add: "Any time you feel tense, just return to the breath. If the movement doesn't come, we can try again later."

Often a student finds the outlines of the movement and with a few adjustments can do it, and continue. Resting in stillness gives us space and time to let emerge what we have learned. In this way of working, the student develops a sense of trust in his own capacity to be a reservoir of the t'ai chi form. The sense of responsibility in learning and teaching shifts from a passive give-and-take between teacher and student to an active exchange. Learning becomes like a strong wind breathing across the ocean. The teacher may blow, but it is the student who catches the wind and sails away magnificently.

Master Benjamin Pang Jeng Lo, a well-known t'ai chi teacher, expressed this view when asked by a journalist to share a secret he had learned during all his years of study. He answered, "The teacher can only show you how to do it. The rest is all your work. The secret is to practice."[1]

Until we have the experience of forgetting a move, we're always afraid it will happen. But when we falter and move through the stuckness, we know it is possible to work with it. Forgetting a move is no longer an impossible challenge but an opportunity to find the secret that Master Lo talks about.

M. Scott Peck writes about this in his book *The Road Less Traveled.*

> What makes life difficult is that the process of confronting and solving problems is a painful one. . . . And since life poses an endless series of problems, life is always difficult and is full of pain as well as joy. Yet it is in this whole process of meeting and solving problems that life has its meaning. . . . Problems call forth our courage and our wisdom; indeed, they create our courage and our wisdom. It is only because of problems that we grow mentally and spiritually. When we desire to encourage the growth of the human spirit, we challenge and encourage the human capacity to solve problems. . . . [I]t is through the pain of confronting and resolving problems that we learn.[2]

To begin practicing even when you have forgotten a move is like throwing a bucket into the well of your own knowledge and experience. Pull up the bucket with trust, knowing that whatever is sitting inside belongs to the process and can be helpful. If you look closely, there's a whole world of encouragement and possibility under the dark murky surface of the deep, deep well.

22

Water Babes

Before my parents bought a house in the Bronx, we used to spend almost every summer at a camp community in New Jersey where we were members. My parents rented a bungalow that felt like a castle compared with the two-room Manhattan apartment shared by my parents, my brother, and me. Every summer morning, promptly at 8:30 A.M., my brother and I left our summer palace to join the streams of children flowing into the community's day-camp program.

We were divided according to age groups. Although I enjoyed the younger group in which I was placed, I envied the older kids—and my brother—who got to do a lot more adventurous things. But I was willing to sacrifice all that in order to keep something that was denied to them because they were over twelve: I was a Water Babe. There was nothing—even if it meant my being eleven years old for the rest of my life—and no one, even if my parents disowned me, that or who could, would, or dared take that status away from me.

The Water Babes, a corps de swim ballet, was the name I gave to our group. It was the creation of John, our three-hundred-pound-plus lifeguard. John was taskmaster and shaman, big, bawdy, and beloved. He was the director of a series of water ballets whose performances on Labor Day became the glorious finale of the camp season for many years. His jumps from the high diving board, in which he curled himself up like a huge cannonball to create a splash so big all the hundreds of onlookers would be drenched, were the high point of our shows.

John was my first t'ai chi teacher; he truly practiced and taught us the watercourse way. He was determined to instill some grace into a bunch of scruffy, pig-tailed waifs. We, the Water Babes, were his life project.

"You are a star, baby," John would yell at us across the water from his director's post, and we would jump into the water thrilled to begin practice. The joy of hearing his praise was so complete that every last little Babe would plunge in, even though the pool was often occupied by a few harmless water snakes.

John taught me how to swim by awakening my joy of moving in water. "The water is your magic carpet, darling," he would sing. "Let it transport you to the heights of ecstasy." Of course, I didn't know what ecstasy was, but if it felt as good as what I was doing, I was ready to go there.

Backstroke, breaststroke, the crawl, it didn't matter what we were doing. John taught us to swim luxuriously, as if we were lolling in a tropical pool covered with water lilies. He even created a chant that we recited with each stroke: "Take your time, take your pleasure. Let it flow. Let it go." Every word of this cadence, our swim master's mantra, accompanied our stretched-out strokes.

John taught me to trust the water and to trust myself. Even with my skinny arms and rather weak legs I could move with grace and effortlessly hold my position with honor in the petal formation that closed every ballet.

John helped us young Babes transcend timidness, low self-esteem, shame about budding breasts or knobby knees. According to him, every part of our body was given to us by God to help us swim. "Don't hide them, darling," John would tell Maria, who would cross her arms across her chest whenever she was out of the water. "Cherish them! They help you float!" Off came the chest wraps and too-tight bras some of us already wore in an American version of Chinese foot binding. For the summer at least, a lot of us could breathe easier and be satisfied with our bodies, no matter what size or shape we were.

John taught us to reach out as far as we could with our strokes. He cajoled us to develop the muscles in our legs so we could kick better. He insisted that we be totally present in every movement we made, in contact with ourselves but also aware of each other. There was no leading Babe in our performances. "Each one of you is part of the whole thing," he would say. "There are no shooting stars in this universe. We are just one biiiiiiiig . . . Milky Way."

John made precision effortless: Although we rehearsed a great deal, there was never a sense of drudgery. The secret of this effortlessness was his teaching us that we were not separate from the water. "You wouldn't fight your foot or arm, would you?" he told us. "Then don't fight the water. Let it carry you."

And for any Babe who was timid about swimming or afraid of drowning, John would say, "Just think you are water, honey. Then you can't drown. How can water sink in water?" he would ask triumphantly.

Many years later, after I had been practicing t'ai chi for some time, I read that it is sometimes described as "swimming in the air." Suddenly so many things that had eluded

me before made sense. I applied what I had learned as a
Water Babe, and my t'ai chi began to feel different.

John taught us to swim long and to let our arms extend
into the water. In t'ai chi I often had difficulty extending, as
if I were afraid to reach out too far. I began to apply what I
had learned during John's lessons. I found I could reach out
much farther than before. I felt more room in my own body
and in the space around me. Most important, I was no longer
afraid either to extend myself or to claim what was mine: the
freedom to move without fear.

One day I tried to do t'ai chi in the water. I went to an
area of the pool where I could stand, and began the form. I
didn't have a weighted belt on and so, although I began with
my feet touching bottom, I was soon floating away. At that
moment I realized how important it was to feel our connection to the ground when doing the form. We often tend to be
focused on arm movements; our fascination with their beauty
causes us to lose our rooting. Being able to feel the ground
through our feet and feel rooted in the earth is one of the
most important t'ai chi principles that we can practice.

John taught us to trust the water and to trust ourselves.
When he showed us a new routine, we always had a period
when we could try things out. He never told us something
was wrong, but rather he would skillfully guide us to streamline a move until it eventually fit into what he wanted us to
do. Every practice session ended with a sense of accomplishment, even if we hadn't quite gotten it together. Rather than
force us to mimic each other so that we would move precisely together, he taught us to be sensitive to and aware of
the person before and behind us, to the left and to the right.
His teaching was creative and creating. It was nurturing in
the truest and most unselfish sense of the word.

One day, as we practiced, I just couldn't understand a move John wanted us to do. After numerous failures, I swam away from the others, climbed out of the water, and ran away. I hid behind a boulder and began crying hard.

Suddenly John was standing in front of me. Despite his bulk, he moved incredibly fast. He kneeled down in front of me.

"What's wrong, honey?" he asked kindly.

"I can't do it. I'm messing up everything. I guess you're going to have to kick me out." I began crying again, desperate at the thought of having to leave the Water Babes.

"Has anyone ever been thrown out of this group?" he asked. I didn't really know. I just looked at him and shrugged my shoulders.

"Well," he said quietly, "no one ever has. The only way you'll be out of this group is by growing out of it."

"I'm messing up the whole thing."

"You ain't messing up nothing, sweetie. You're just being creative, kind of experimenting with things. You need a bit more playing with it until it feels right."

"The others are mad at me."

"They're not mad; they're just a bit impatient. . . . But don't you worry. We are going to keep practicing and keep trying. This isn't about getting things right. It's about your loving swimming and loving yourself. Don't beat up on yourself. We just have to keep experimenting until we find the routine that's right for all you Babes."

The next day I dragged my feet as I headed toward the pool. It wasn't fun to be a Water Babe that day. I knew John wanted to rehearse the part that I had trouble with. After our usual warm-up, we began to practice the troublesome routine. Just as we got to the part I couldn't do, John stopped us and told us to gather round.

"We were working on this part yesterday," he began, "and one of you Babes seemed to be really into it. In fact, you were doing something really great. After sleeping on it, I've decided that it's a lot more interesting than what we've been doing. So we're going to incorporate those new moves into the routine." I looked toward John with a big smile on my face. He gave me a thumbs-up.

Over the next few days, John continued to modify the routine, including the part that I had choreographed. I moved easily with the changes, and our troupe was soon performing the routine as if we had been doing it for years. It turned out to be exactly what he had wanted in the first place, only he took a roundabout way to get there.

I remembered John's lesson about roundaboutness many times in the years to come, not only as a student but also as a teacher. It helped me to understand, for example, why some students are afraid to practice at home: they are afraid of not getting a movement right. "Right" means doing it exactly as they were taught in class. So rather than risk any deviation, a student won't practice at all. The next time he goes to class, he'll have to begin all over again.

Practicing a new movement is like making a drawing. Most artists begin by first sketching the outline roughly. They stand away from it, make changes, and when they are satisfied, they begin filling in the details. It's the same with each new movement. You have begun to sketch the movement in class, and at home you continue to work on your outline. When you return to class, the combination of your own practice and input from your teacher and classmates helps you to fill in the details and make things more precise.

If there's no frame in the first place, then any adjustments are like doodling in empty space.

Be aware of the quality of your movement when you practice something new. Does it feel as if you were lugging a ball and chain, as if you were imprisoning yourself in the form? Are you rehearsing to be a bomb expert, gingerly carrying a device that seems like it could explode at any moment? Are you tying yourself up in a straitjacket woven from your fear of criticism—or fear of freedom?

When you notice that kind of tightness, then becoming aware of it is the first big step toward releasing it. Take a deep breath, stretch a bit, and just pick up the form as if you were going to dance with a child. Give yourself permission to play, to roll with, to stretch, to exaggerate, to be as roundabout as you need to be. Be a T'ai Chi Babe.

Exercises

REACHING OUT, EXTENDING OUR ENERGY

The purpose of this exercise is to encourage you to circulate your chi, or vital energy, and to let it flow freely through the body. It is also meant to help you to develop your intention in sensing and moving the chi, as well as extending it beyond the limits of your body.[1]

If the word *chi* is not something that you relate to, then think of the exercise as a kind of internal and external stretching. The muscles and ligaments feel this tug, which also helps to stimulate blood flow and muscle tonus. It also aids to release the crampedness in our movements and to extend our presence into the world around us.

In t'ai chi we talk about drawing energy from the root. In an oft-quoted line from the *T'ai Chi Ch'uan Ching*, a classical t'ai chi text attributed to Chang San-feng, it says: "The motion should be rooted in the feet, released through the legs, controlled by the waist and manifested through the fingers."[2] This sense of being connected to the ground and yet also experiencing a lightness of movement has a wonderful quality to it. When we have a sense of it, we can dance like a tree in the wind, our branches tossing lightly as our deep roots keep us bound to the earth.

Begin the exercise by standing with your feet parallel and shoulder-width apart. Your hands are lying on top of each other in the middle of the lower belly just under the navel. Stand quietly for about one minute. Then separate the hands and bring your arms to rest by your sides, the palms facing the body.

We begin the exercise on the left side. Extend the fingers of your left hand as if you wanted to touch the ground. It helps to imagine that someone is pulling lightly on your fingers (the shoulders remain at the same height). Take your time with the exercise and feel the stretch to a limit that is comfortable but nevertheless extended. After one minute, let the arm rest at your side. Take a moment to sense how your arm feels now compared with the way it did in the beginning.

Lift your left arm in front of you to shoulder height. Imagine there is a wall or tree in front of you, for example, and you want to touch it with your fingertips. The shoulders remain on the same plane. After one minute, slowly lower your arm.

Lift the left arm above your head and reach up as if you wish to touch the ceiling. Take your time and feel the stretch. Do not raise your left shoulder above the right one. Then slowly lower your arm to your side. Stand for some moments in stillness.

Raise your left arm out to the side at shoulder height. Reach out with your fingers as if you wish to touch a wall (do no lean to the left). Then slowly lower your arm to your side.

Take a moment to sense your left arm and how it feels, especially in relation to the right one.

Repeat the exercise with the right arm in the same sequence: reaching downward, in front of you, above the head, and out to the sides.

Finish the exercise by standing quietly with your arms at your side. Then place one hand over the other on your abdomen. Stand until you sense a natural end to the exercise. You may end with the massage described at the end of Preparation.

Variation 1

The exercise can be repeated, but this time begin by standing with the left foot one step forward and pointing straight ahead. The right foot is turned in approximately a forty-five-degree angle to the right.

Repeat the exercise in exactly the same sequence as before. Now, however, as you reach forward you can turn the body to the right and at the same time reach forward with your left arm. Turning the body will allow you to reach forward more. But be careful not to extend the knee over the foot. Continue slowly and take the time to sense how your left arm feels after reaching in each direction.

Repeat the exercise with the right arm and the right foot forward. End the exercise as described earlier.

Application within the T'ai Chi Form

Do your form slowly and notice especially in what movements you can reach out. Try to continue the careful attention that you developed during the exercise to sense what is going on during the form. Don't rush through the movements. Feel the movement internally as well as externally.

With a Partner

Do the t'ai chi form and stop after every movement. Have a partner lightly pull your fingers to help you to experience the feeling of stretching. Stay in your center and do not let your partner pull you out of the posture. Let your awareness rest in your back and legs and feet and sense the movements extending from your feet. Explore all the form movements for the quality of extension, not just the ones in which it seems obvious.

The Heart of Practice

This exercise is not only about experiencing the sense of reaching out but also about maintaining a sense of dignity and eloquence in our movements. In some ways it feels as if we are dancing with our arms stretched wide, but we are grounded and deeply connected to the earth.

We tend to be frontally oriented when doing the form, but when we move with a sense of our back as well as our front, the movements have much more substance and engage the whole body. We touch all the directions when we move or stand, and this gives us breadth, height, and depth.

The exercise also helps us to develop an internal attention. It asks us to relate to the outside and to the inside with the same sense of wakefulness and care. It is a wonderful opportunity to be in touch with ourselves in a way that is deeply nourishing. And to be able to extend in all directions, even to get the needle at the bottom of the sea.

Fair Lady at the Shuttle

The movement called Fair Lady at the Shuttle is impossible to describe in a few words because it comprises four movements. For those who are interested in a more precise description, I refer them to Master William C. C. Chen's book *Body Mechanics of T'ai Chi Chuan*. However, here I would like to share some associations I have with the movement, which is one of my favorites.

Fair Lady involves our doing similar movements to four directions. The footwork, as well as the arm movements, is complicated, and so Fair Lady presents us with quite a challenge in terms of executing it smoothly. One image that suggests the smoothness with which we can do Fair Lady is that of spinning wool.

In a living-museum village near La Martinie, our retreat center in southwest France, an elder gives demonstrations of wool spinning that mesmerize young and old. Her work is captivating not because she is doing anything spectacular but because her smoothness, tenderness, and fierce concentration, all rolled into one, leave the crowd breathless. One day she explained to me how spinning wool is a metaphor for living one's life. "The tension with which you hold the wool must be exactly right," she said. "If you jerk on it, the wool breaks. If you're too careful and hold on too tight, the wool also breaks. If you're too lax, the wool spins into a mess . . . *comme la vie!*" she added, with a quixotic smile.

Fair Lady also asks for our full engagement and sensitivity

to the right touch. As we move from direction to direction there is the sense of weaving with a fine thread, as if we were creating the most beautiful tapestry with our movements.

Fair Lady also has a quality that suggests the ebb and flow of tides. At the end of each of the four corners we are standing as if we were pushing something away, or as if the tide had flowed onto the beach. But to go on to the next corner we must first flow backward like the ebb of a tide, to gather ourselves again so that we can pour ourselves into the next wave.

The next time you are near the ocean, let the waves inspire you. If you know t'ai chi, do the form as if you were being moved by the motions of the waves. If you don't know the form, stand at the shore until you feel the rhythm of the ocean, and allow it to infuse you. Lightly buoyant, roiling, crashing to the shore, all movements of the ocean are contained in this dance of tides.

23

True Grit

Iron and Silk, by Mark Salzman, tells the story of the author's
stay in China during a stint of teaching English. The book
also chronicles his study of *wu shu* (martial arts) under a Chinese master. I recommend the book to all my students, not
only because it gives a good picture of Chinese society on a
day-to-day level, but also because Mark's training in wu shu
serves as an example of the highs and lows of what can happen when we learn these arts, including t'ai chi.

There is one section that I am particularly fond of. Mark
is visiting his teacher, who is the trainer at one of China's
magnet wu shu schools. The students are drawn from all over
the country to train for competition and performance in the
martial arts. They enter at a very young age, after being se-
lected by visiting teams and by local sports officials. While it
is certainly an honor to be chosen, and for some students
from poor families, a golden opportunity, the curriculum is
famous for being grueling. Often, for at least ten years of
their lives, the pupils are immersed in a training program
that involves morning-to-night study, either in the classroom
or in the gymnasium. Their teachers expect unquestioned
compliance and obedience. As the following excerpt shows,

the students literally place their lives in the hands of their teachers.

Two students are practicing a combat routine with weapons. Master Pan, Mark Salzman's teacher, watches them with a steely eye, obviously not satisfied. The author describes what happens next:

> They tried again, but still Pan growled angrily. Suddenly he got up and took the dadao [a broadsword attached to a thick wooden pole] from the first woman. The entire training hall went silent and still. Without warming up at all, Pan ordered the woman with the spear to get ready, and to move fast when the time came. His body looked as though electricity had suddenly passed through it, and the huge blade flashed toward her. Once, twice the dadao flew beneath her feet, then swung around in a terrible arc and rode her back with flawless precision. The third time he added a little twist at the end so that the blade grazed up her neck and sent a little decoration stuck in her pigtails flying across the room.
>
> I had to sit down for a moment to ponder the difficulty of sending an object roughly the shape of an oversized shovel only heavier, across a girl's back and through her pigtails, without guide ropes or even a safety helmet. . . . Pan handed the dadao back to the woman and walked over to me.
>
> "What if you had made a mistake?" I asked.
>
> "I never make mistakes," he said, without looking at me.[1]

My students react in two general ways when I read this part of the book to them. Either they are impressed or they find the teacher brutal.

Those who like the story, seem to think of Master Pan as China's answer to John Wayne. It's the coolness, I think. Just picture John Wayne standing in the middle of the circled wagon train as it is attacked by Indians. Everyone is in a panic; yet when he takes charge, it's as if the Fifth Cavalry had arrived. We can still hear those trumpets blasting at us from our childhood stints in front of the TV watching the late movie.

What is really cool about John Wayne? Well, he got the job done, didn't he? Always! And he encouraged those around him to get their jobs done. He had a kind of dig-your-heels-in, bite-the-bullet attitude, and whether we like it or not, his image has influenced the American idea of a hero. Whatever these characters do, they do it 100 percent. They give of themselves completely and they expect others to give completely. They're the kind of people the following catchphrase was written for: "When the going gets tough, the tough get going."

Those who don't like the story say that Master Pan is an example of a cold, distant educator who is interested only in results. He exemplifies the worst of a paternalistic authority figure. He sacrifices his students' humanity and expects them to perform like war machines: faceless and merciless. "My God, these are children," one student began, "where is their childhood? And where are their rights?" These people do not think Master Pan is cool. They think he should be denied tenure.

I bring up this story, not to get lost in the pros and cons of humanistic versus militaristic education, but to raise an issue that I have observed over and over again in the nineteen years I have been teaching t'ai chi. In fact, this observation goes back more than thirty years, to my days as a student teacher of high school English.

We learn something when we are challenged to stretch beyond what we think our boundaries are. When we are always working at a level that seems comfortable, we tend to stagnate. When we are not challenged, whatever we do learn soon fades. When we always perform at a chugging pace, our faces never know what it is to glow with joy.

There is a famous picture of Princess Diana that expresses beautifully the joy and excitement of being challenged. The photo shows her running in a race with other mothers at her son's school. In the photo Diana is just about to cross the finish line as the winner. Obviously she is running full out. Princess or not, she's kicked off her shoes and given this race everything she's got. Her face flashes a radiant smile. But she's not smiling because of all the cheers at the sideline. She's a princess; she's used to that. It's because the cheers around her are really echoes of the cheers inside her. Her effort is just one big *yes!* She's right there, giving 100 percent of herself.

The kind of spirit I'm talking about can be described as a willingness to engage the moment with all the resources we have. It means that we allow ourselves to be curious, even playful, when learning the form, like a puppy who is over-joyed to find an unguarded slipper after everyone has gone to bed. When you learn a new move, try not to rush to get it down pat. Sniff it, toss it around a bit, let it slowly find its shape. Instead of attacking a move as if it were an obstinate nail you want to drive into the wall, savor it as you would fine wine. While you may not always feel this way, especially at the end of a long day when you would rather be soaking in a hot bath than training in a cold gymnasium, it is possible to raise this kind of quiet determination to make the most of every moment.

Recently I was invited to teach a saber workshop on an island in the Mediterranean off the coast of Spain. The teacher who invited me had graciously arranged for the workshop and encouraged her students to come along. Not knowing a weapons form herself, she wanted to give her advanced students an opportunity to stretch their knowledge of t'ai chi, as well as satisfy her long-standing desire to learn the saber form.

Normally I do not like to teach a whole form in two weekends, but this was a special exception. The island the teacher and students live on is not exactly around the corner from me. And they had arranged to practice together every week, so I knew they would have the combined knowledge of the group to rely on, rather than each person being left alone to flounder. But what reassured me the most was the spirit and focus with which the students applied themselves. They gave complete attention and dedication to learning each move, exploring it and practicing it over and over again. We moved fluidly through the form, and though we accomplished a great deal, I never had the feeling we rushed through it.

Each person was very different, and yet they all gave entirely of themselves. Some were fast learners, some slower, some could mirror me exactly, others took a longer time to hone a movement until it came close to what I had demonstrated. Some people had a strong sense of themselves; others were less sure and expressed themselves more quietly. Each person had his own way of giving completely, which expressed itself beautifully throughout the weekend, like a vast web being woven by many different spiders and yet all linked together by a common effort.

The secret of giving 100 percent is really that we give everything in the moment or activity. Normally we think that giving everything means having to make a big effort, usually one that involves a lot of muscle. But when we are completely present, it is effortless. Giving, or surrendering to the moment, often means letting go of all the thoughts and dialogue that usually get in the way of just being present. The most frequent thoughts that fill our moments are usually all the reasons that we simply can't do something. They are reasons that have been drilled into us or come from an insecure place within ourselves. But when we just give ourselves the chance to move, the body has a wisdom of its own. It knows how to measure our energy and pace—and how to get us to let go.

True grit is not the province only of John Wayne, Sylvester Stallone, GI Jane, or wu shu teachers. It's also the mettle of the t'ai chi lady at Fourth and Pine practicing her form each morning in the playground, her sneakers slowly rubbing the pavement into polished stone.

24
Just Stand Up!

About ten years ago I was meeting a group of students for the eighth weekend of a nine-weekend series. For any group to learn the form in nine weekends requires that I stick to a fairly strict schedule. On this weekend I had planned for them to learn the movement Fair Lady, as well as to review what they had done before. While I always allow extra time for variations in learning speeds, this particular group was dragging its heels considerably. I sensed that their languid pace was not so much because they learned slowly as that they had not yet committed as a group to the process for which they had signed up.

I was unsure how to proceed. I knew they needed to make a very strong effort if they were to finish on schedule. On the other hand, I was not sure they could increase their effort to the level necessary. I decided to explain the situation to the group and let them decide how we should continue.

Basically, I presented two options. One was that we could drop the goal of learning the entire form by the end of the ninth weekend and just proceed at a slower pace. If they decided to finish, however, then we needed to make a contract: in return for my teaching them at a speed that would enable them to finish, they would have to train and practice at a much more intense level than previously.

After some discussion, the group agreed unanimously to finish the form. I repeated the terms of the contract, and especially the mandate they had given me to teach at whatever speed I deemed necessary. For their part, they agreed to match my pace.

By the end of the first day, each and every participant was exhausted. When they returned on Sunday morning, I sensed it was going to be a tough day. I purposely dove into training rather than checking in with each of them in our usual morning round. I had a feeling it would not help things if they were to give too much space to their tiredness at this point.

At the midmorning break they collapsed on the floor. The usual rush for beverages or the toilet was all but stilled. After a short break, I called them together to practice. To the last person they stared back at me defiantly.

"Can't we take a longer break?" one woman asked between clenched teeth. The others stared at me with just as fierce a determination to remain glued to the floor.

"Do you remember our discussion yesterday?" I asked.

"I'd rather not," said one of the women humorlessly.

"Just to refresh all our memories, I'll repeat the gist of it." I then reviewed our discussion and finished with the statement that we had made a contract.

"Yes, you're right," said a man. "But can't we just rest a little bit longer now? We can make up for it later."

I decided to lay it on the line there and then. "Do you want to finish the form or not?" I asked directly.

"Yes," several replied.

"Then just stand up!" I said sharply. I felt a kind of shock wave ripple through the group. I moved to the front and took my place, ready to begin.

Within a few moments, the group fell into place behind me. We finished what we needed to accomplish that weekend. And in the next, we finished the form.

At the end of the last weekend of the series, we took time for all the students to reflect on the eight months they had spent learning the form.

"I felt like I received an electric shock when you told us to stand up," one man said. "At that moment I knew the choice was all mine. And no matter what I chose, I, and not anyone else, would have to stand up for it."

"I was angry," said another woman. "I thought you were the worst sadist I had ever met. I wanted to get up and bury you under all those books in your library. But as I stood up, I reflected on what I was feeling. If I could take that energy and put it into my form, rather than throwing it at you, then maybe I could get something done."

"I only got up because the rest of you got up," said another woman. "I was so tired I didn't feel either resistance or anger. I just put one foot in front of the other. Actually, it felt like I kind of surrendered and gave everything up to the universe."

The kind of attitude that is implied in the words *Just stand up!* is not a grim, gritted-teeth determination with which we power ourselves to face a situation at all odds. There is nothing grim about accepting the invitation that life offers us in so many situations to go deep and make good on the promises we made to ourselves earlier. Honoring our commitment not only to others but to ourselves is in fact to express what Chögyam Trungpa called fearlessness. It is not based on a harder-than-hard clenching up but on a gentle opening that reveals a strong core. Chögyam Trungpa writes in *Shambhala:*

The Sacred Path of the Warrior: "Real fearlessness is the product of tenderness. It comes from letting the world tickle your heart, your raw and beautiful heart. You are willing to open up, without resistance or shyness, and face the world. You are willing to share your heart with others."[1]

And with yourself!

25

Stillness in Movement

The stillness in stillness is not the real stillness.
Only when there is stillness in movement
Can the spiritual rhythm appear which pervades heaven and earth.

—Ts'ai-ken t'an

When I first read this verse[1] of the ancient Chinese sage Ts'ai-ken t'an, I felt they were the most meaningful words to describe t'ai chi that I knew of. But like all such words of depth, they were not so clear. I knew that he wrote them based on what he had experienced, so what was it behind the words? That question was to be the base of my entire training and later flowed into my teaching.

I once led a group of advanced t'ai chi students in an exercise that was to illuminate Ts'ai-ken t'an's words and leave a very deep impression on all of us. As it sometimes is with a revealing exercise, I had not planned it beforehand.

We were practicing Fair Lady at the Shuttle, a movement also known as Four Corners because it is done to the northwest, southwest, northeast, and southeast. I suddenly had the idea that we should do Four Corners over and over again, without a time limit, until things came to a natural halt. I had never done such an exercise before, and we all began enthusiastically.

The first twenty minutes went fine. After that people became visibly tired. As we continued, many of us could hardly pick up our arms. I kept wondering when we would fall apart as a group. I knew that if one person faltered, then all of us would follow suit.

At some point I became so tired I began to lose a sense of where I was. Just as I was about to stop, I felt a wave of quiet energy fill my body. I lost all sense that I was doing the form. It was just happening: there was no me controlling or determining the movements. My eyes settled on other people around me. We had become so harmonized in our actions that without our trying, our movements were completely synchronized. It felt as if we were riding the same wave.

We did Fair Lady for forty minutes. When we stopped, which seemed to happen naturally, we all felt refreshed and vibrant.

In the exchange that followed, someone said: "I have read the words *wu wei,* or effortless power, so many times in connection with t'ai chi. But I have to admit that I was always puzzled by the idea of 'nondoing.' Now I know that I was getting hung up on the words. This experience is beyond words."

Someone else added, "I don't know what happened as we were doing Fair Lady. I can't find the words for it either. But I do feel at some point that all resistance flowed out of me. When I thought I couldn't make it any further, I gave up trying to force myself. And in that moment, something carried me."

The stillness that we found within the movement was our own nonstriving. So long as we were pushing to reach a goal, we carried ourselves with tension, and we were focused very tightly on ourselves. When we relaxed into the tiredness, basically because we had no choice, then the preoccupation with our goals, self-interest, everything to do with strengthening our sense of individual identity, just relaxed. With that a deeper sense of energy became available to us that carried us through the exercise.

T'ai chi is only one of countless movement rituals that can be described as meditation in movement. These movement rituals, many of which are dance or martial arts forms, allow us to empty ourselves of self, or our sense of personality, by giving us an opportunity to put ourselves into something completely. When we do, there is just the movement, just the step, no one special is doing the form.

Zen teacher Dennis Genpo Merzel, Roshi, describes it this way:

When we go into any activity, work, or play, if we really put ourselves into it completely, not holding back even one percent, doing it with compete faith and determination and throwing ourselves into it, then we disappear. Then in our very movement there is stillness, peace of mind. . . . When we are totally engaged, we are completely still within the activity. There is complete silence and in that silence there is no self, no *I*. That is why in all religions throughout the ages mystics have sought after inner silence, the still point. In that very quietness there is no thought. When there is no thought, then there is no *me*, no self.[2]

T'ai chi is an opportunity to open to the spiritual rhythm that is present in every moment. Most of the time we are too busy doing something and often forcing something to happen to allow ourselves to sense it. Letting go of our ideas, plans, ambitions, or self-judgments, even for a second, allows the natural rhythm of life to be present as it is, before we make so much effort to shape, curtail, streamline, and, above all, control it.

The spiritual rhythm flows deep and through every one of us. It flows through every moment of life. In the t'ai chi form each moment is pregnant with it. Some call it the Tao, others call it the movement of the spheres; Christians call it grace, modern psychology calls it flow. It is the baseline rhythm present in the midst of all the other rhythms in the universe: of peace and quietness, of turbulence and storms, of a baby's burbling coo and an adult daughter's efforts to help her aged father stand on shaky legs. It is the subtle movement of the stars on a dark night and the full-out tilt of a young child participating in her first school race.

Jerky and unsure, flowing and elegant, it is embodied by a t'ai chi player without arms and a t'ai chi player who soars to the height of mastery. It is Lilly, our young Labrador, snapping up her head to nab a fly. It is a scientist watching quarks shimmer through an electron microscope. It's a young couple in a French café playing cards, and a kung fu pinball machine spitting out grunts and flashing the shifty eyes of a martial arts hunk. It's an old man sitting in a cave on one side of the world reciting sutras. It's a mother on the other side of the world watching her daughter step up to receive her college diploma as her tears water the roses she holds close to her breasts, like the baby she held so many years earlier.

What is not dancing to the spiritual rhythm of heaven and

earth? What is not pervaded by it? The next time you do your t'ai chi form, dance, vacuum the living room, ski, swim, or carry the bags from the supermarket to the car, find the stillness in movement. Let go into the moment, as it is, and just be there, as you are. Then you will know there is nothing to find because you never lost it.

Let your smile pervade heaven and earth.

26

Fair Lady Sowing Seeds

Just as we would not expect a full-grown sunflower to appear the morning after we had planted its seed, neither is it possible to do the t'ai chi movements exactly like our teacher the moment after we have seen them for the first time. Yet so many of us get frustrated when we can't reproduce a movement exactly the way we have been shown. If we were planting a garden, we would be the type of person who lays down ready-made sod and plants very large trees.

Impatient gardeners and some t'ai chi practitioners have one thing in common: a lack of faith in the natural process of growth. It's the kind of attitude that leads us to get fed up when we don't have a move down perfectly by the end of class. When students express this to me, I tell them to ask themselves one question: "What's the rush?"

Seeds grow best in a garden where the earth has been prepared and they are allowed to develop naturally: the soil has been turned over for aeration, the weeds have been removed, and a good layer of compost has been spread on the surface. In such a soil, seeds take root quickly, though it may be quite some time before they can burst forth in all their glory.

I have found that it is much easier to teach a movement

when there is time for it to germinate, if only for a short while. For example, sometimes when a class is nearly over, I introduce students to a new movement. There is usually only enough time for explaining the move and going through it a few times.

Sometimes a student asks me not to go on because she says she won't remember the movement after such a short acquaintance. My response is to invite her to treat the process as an experiment. "See if you can let go of the need to 'get' the movement and just be curious about what will happen." I tell her we will go into more depth with the movement the next time we meet, whether it is after the lunch break or a month later.

When we work on the movement again, the student has already absorbed some of the shape and nuances of it, even if she's not aware of it. After a few repetitions, I send her off to practice on her own. Now, rather than opening the door to a newcomer, practicing the movement feels like welcoming an old friend one hasn't seen in a while.

It's almost as if the body is like a sponge when we learn the form. When a sponge is completely dry, it does not absorb liquid well. First it has to be soaked and wrung out and then it absorbs much better. So, too, with the t'ai chi form. When we return to the movement again, after being briefly immersed in it, we absorb it with more ease. And though it may not yet have permeated to the bones, the movement is no longer on the surface.

There is a similar process that happens as we advance in the form. In the course of studying the first part of the form, we have not only been learning the movements but have also been learning how to learn. Our powers of observation have been sharpened, our capacity to reproduce what we see has been refined, and even new movements have qualities of what we already know, so they are not completely foreign.

To foster this process, I always ask my students to sit down and watch me demonstrate a new movement. Usually I do a move five times before saying anything. I learned this technique from my chi kung teacher, Master B. P. Chan. He used to tell us that we should watch each part of his body when he demonstrated a move. We should look at his feet, waist, hands, upper body, and then his whole body. It was not easy to focus in such a detailed way, but with time I developed somewhat of an eagle eye. It was to stand me in good stead in later years when I began teaching.

I ask my students to sit down because if they don't, most of them begin mimicking the movements immediately. We are not paying attention in a focused way when we do this. And we are not training our powers of observation. We are, instead, fostering a kind of hurry-up attitude, one that demands swift gratification. The swiftness guarantees in turn that we will not be satisfied for long. We begin searching again, not realizing that the need for speed and the inability to savor are the causes of the problem.

When we watch with a kind of careful attention, we are watering the soil and preparing for the seed to be planted. It is one of the reasons I tell my students that rather than leave the room if they are tired, they should sit down and watch. I know from my own experience that stepping out of a group class to watch my teacher and classmates was a very important part of my training. If I didn't understand a move, I would move to an angle where I could see clearly and then focus carefully on whatever section was troubling me. Usually I had to watch several times, but when I saw what I needed to see, it was as if something dropped into place.

When you plant seeds, there is no absolute guarantee you are going to get exactly what is pictured on the packet. All sorts of things influence the growth process: the length of the growing season, the amount of rainfall and sunlight, how much fertilizer you use, the number of slugs, bugs, and snails that take up residence in your flower patch. According to my husband, an avid gardener, that's the joy of the whole thing. Every spring he takes morning strolls in his garden just before breakfast to peruse his landscape of wonder. From day to day there can be immense changes—if one is paying attention—and the mystery is in not knowing what will happen next.

27

Pang

There are many stories in both modern and ancient cultures on the most skillful ways that a student can train in something. One of the first films produced by the People's Republic of China, *The Undaunted Wu Dang*, (1994), is particularly interesting for t'ai chi practitioners in this respect. It tells the story of a young woman, already an extraordinary fighter, who seeks to find and punish the murderers of her father, a patriot and renowned martial artist. Perplexed about her own skills after she loses a fight against one of the murderers, she seeks out her father's only remaining training brother, a Taoist master who lives in a beautiful mountain temple. He tells her that the reason she has failed is that she does not yet embody the principle of the soft overcoming the hard. But before he can teach her, he goes on, she must be willing to begin at the beginning and forget all she knows. And she must continue training, whatever happens.

The Undaunted Wu Dang is actually a reworking of a traditional story found in many versions in Buddhist and Asian cultures. A famous example of it in Tibetan Buddhist culture is the story of Milarepa, whose teacher, Marpa, makes him build a tower, knock it down, and build it again and again until he is satisfied that his student has been emptied of pride and arrogance. I recently found a modern version of this story in a Chinese children's book titled *Lui Ban Learns His Craft*. It involves a young carpentry apprentice who must build house after house until his teacher is satisfied that he can do it with his eyes closed.

I would like to share my own version of this classic motif in the following story about a young woman named Pang. It is the kind of archetypical story in which each reader can find personal themes. For some people, the story may not seem relevant within a twenty-first-century Western person's cultural framework, as one of my students suggests, but I believe the story is very rich in symbolism. I encourage you to let both the person in you who nods in agreement and the person in you who feels some resistance to have a say. Only then can the tale really shine as a teaching story.

There was once a young woman named Pang who wanted to learn the martial arts. A teacher accepted her into his school and she applied herself wholeheartedly. She was a talented student and learned quickly. As soon as she finished one form, she went to her teacher and begged him to teach her something new. In this way she was able to learn many forms in a short time. She was also an excellent fighter. She trained just like everyone else and refused to allow others not to train seriously with her because she was a woman. After several years her teacher called her to him.

"You have been a dedicated student. You have accomplished in a short time what others do not accomplish even in twenty years. I would like to make you a teacher. But before I do so, there is one more level of training that you must undergo."

"What can that be, teacher?" Pang answered incredulously. "I don't think there is anything I have missed. If so, please tell me at once so that I can apply myself."

"I am sending you to my sister, Master Lin, in the mountains. You will complete your training with her."

"But you are my teacher, Master. I do not want to train with anyone else."

"Because I am your teacher, you cannot complete this last stage with me. Go now! Learn what you need to learn."

"But what is that, teacher? As far as I know I have learned everything. And how long must I stay with Master Lin?"

Her teacher turned his back, a sign that he had finished the interview. She left the room in a state of complete agitation.

The next day she set out for the mountains. After a long search, she found the hut of her teacher's sister. As Pang approached, Master Lin was sitting at a weaver's loom. She worked the shuttle with a fluidity and speed that Pang had never seen before. The belt she was weaving was the finest Pang had ever seen.

Master Lin told her to set down her belongings in a small hut attached to the house. The hut was simple but sufficient. When Pang returned, there was a plate of steaming food waiting for her.

"We will begin your training tomorrow morning," said Master Lin. "As is my habit, I will now retire to bed." The master turned and entered her home without another word. Pang went to bed that night homesick for her teacher and her training companions.

The next morning Pang woke early and did her training exercises. She was curious what her new teacher would ask of her. After her morning meditation, Master Lin emerged from her hut. She called Pang to her.

"I will now give you an exercise. You must do this for

three hours every morning and every evening. The rest of
the time you may train in the exercises that you have learned
with my brother."

She brought Pang to a part of the compound where there
was a small stream. Master Lin scooped up a handful of mud
out of the riverbed. It was a thick claylike substance. She
formed a small ball with it and then set it on a rock to dry.
She made several of these balls as Pang continued to watch.

"Every morning and every evening you will make these
balls. Make them as firm as you can. The size is whatever
you can hold in one hand."

"How many should I make, teacher?"

"Continue to make them until I tell you to stop."

"When will that be?"

"When it happens." Master Lin turned and walked back to
her hut.

Pang began to make the balls as she had been instructed.
The days, weeks, and months went by. Soon both riverbanks
were covered with balls.

Several times she approached Master Lin at her loom to
ask if she had made enough balls. Each time the teacher did
not answer but continued with her weaving. At one point
Pang became very angry.

"I am wasting my time," she said to herself. "There is no
reason to make all these balls. They are not even useful."

One day Master Lin announced, "I am changing your exercise. From now on you are to take one ball in each hand
and squeeze it into dust."

Pang was shocked. After all that work, Master Lin was now
asking her to destroy it all.

"But I don't understand. What has all this to do with my
training? Please, teacher. Tell me the reason so that I can

understand better." But Master Lin remained silent and continued weaving. Pang knew she must return to her work.

As her hands became stronger, Pang was able to work faster. After some months, she had squeezed all the balls to powder.

One day Master Lin called Pang to her. "Your training is over. Now it is time to return to my brother."

Pang was aghast. "Teacher, I beg you. Please do not send me away without letting me complete my training."

"Your training is finished. Return home and take up the position my brother has intended for you."

"But I cannot until I have finished what I need to learn."

"Your training is over. Leave tomorrow morning at dawn."

In the morning, Pang went to Master Lin to say goodbye. After making her parting bows, Pang was about to leave. Master Lin stepped forward and placed a belt that she had woven around the young woman's waist.

"It has taken twelve months to weave this belt. Let it be a remembrance of the time you have spent here and a sign that you have finished your training." For the first time, she placed her hands on Pang's shoulders and said in a kind voice. "Have no fear. All that you need to know is within you. It will show at the proper time."

Pang left the place where she had spent the past twelve months. Her heart was heavy. She was returning home, she thought, without learning what she had come for. How could she face her teacher and her fellow students?

At that moment a group of bandits surrounded her. How was she to defend herself? She was carrying no weapons. Without thinking she reached up and grabbed a thick branch of a nearby tree. She gave it a slight twist and the branch came away in her hand. She stood quietly, waiting for the bandits to attack.

They were stunned. It would have taken several persons with cutting tools to do what this young woman had accomplished with such ease. She must have supernatural powers! Maybe she was the spirit of someone they had killed who had returned to take revenge. Without a moment's hesitation, they turned and rode away furiously.

Pang stood with the branch in her hands, watching the bandits retreat. When they were out of sight, she lay it against the tree. A feeling of deep gratitude welled up in her. She had a sudden vision of Master Lin sitting in front of her house. She was smiling and nodding her head as she wove at the speed of a shooting star. Pang turned and bowed toward the mountain hermitage of Master Lin and then in the direction of the teacher to whom she was returning.

Finally, she had no more questions.

Exercises

CAN YOU MAKE IT LIGHTER?

I created the following exercise after I saw a video about Mentastics, a system of bodywork developed by Milton Trager. The film pictured Mr. Trager, then in his early eighties, working with a student. One thing that impressed me was the way he stimulated a student to inquire into the nature of her own movements. Over and over he would ask her: "Can you make it lighter?" As the student continued to move, you could see how this kind of questioning was encouraging an internal exploration that indeed resulted in the movements' being more fluid and softer.

But what exactly does Milton Trager mean by *lighter*? I invite you to try the following exercise as a way of discovering the answer for yourself.

Pick a movement from the form that you know well and that you have no problems with. It should be a move where you feel very comfortable and without restriction. If you do not practice t'ai chi or chi kung then create a short sequence on the spot. You can even mime an action from daily life, such as answering the phone or sweeping the floor.

Repeat the movement ten times. Each time you do the movement, be aware of any moment where you feel a heaviness or holding back. Also observe when the move feels light or effortless. What are the principles that seem to determine whether the movement feels light and flowing? Look at things like the width of your stance, the range of movement in the hips, the relaxation of the shoulders, and so forth.

Now choose a move from the form with which you have difficulty or that you know is somehow a problem for you. It can also be an everyday action. Do the movement ten times. First try to sense more exactly at what point you feel a tightness or heaviness. As you move, ask yourself, "Can I make it lighter?" Don't force yourself to find something. Your attention should have a light and delicate quality. If you find that you are getting too insistent about the questioning, back off and take a short break. Then try again.

Variation for Group Practice
The teacher or the group as a whole should choose a movement from a form that each person knows well and has relatively few problems with. Each person should do the movement ten times, observing the principles or things that make it feel light. Gently ask the question: "Can I make it lighter?"

The participants form groups of two. A should choose a movement from the form with which he has difficulty. B observes him as he does the move five times. As B watches, she asks herself: "What is one suggestion I could make to A that would help him do the move more lightly?" It's a good idea to jot this down.

As A does the moves, he should ask himself, "How can I make it lighter?" A should take some moments at the end of the fifth repetition to jot down his own notes.

A presents his ideas to B first. After doing so, A and B compare notes.

A does the movement again, and B makes suggestions on where and how A can adapt what B has seen. Leave time for A and B to discuss and talk about what they have discovered.

When A has finished his movement, A and B switch roles.

Allow enough time for the exercise so that A and B can exchange without feeling any pressure. Then bring the whole group together and let each pair present what they discovered as they did the exercise.

The Heart of Practice

This exercise is valuable for many reasons. For one thing, it trains a kind of careful attention that is soft and yet taking place at a deep level of inquiry. The softness is particularly helpful because it trains a relaxed concentration, two words that when paired together are often difficult for beginning t'ai chi students to embody in their practice.

I usually introduce this exercise after students have learned the form, but not always. Sometimes I do it after they have learned only half of the form. It is encouraging for many people to see that they do indeed know some of the t'ai chi principles, at least theoretically. This kind of practice is stimulating and encourages the students to take an active role in their learning process.

It's also a lot of fun to do this exercise with a partner. It's quite amazing how often A and B have exactly the same suggestions for how a move can be made lighter. Practicing together in a spirit of cooperation establishes a social climate based on mutual support and inquiry. This process does not always flow smoothly at first because most of us have been trained to criticize and not to support. It takes time to learn the difference between assistance and correction.

Can you make it lighter? is a question that doesn't flow only through one's t'ai chi practice. The ripples of this quiet but persistent inquiry can spread to other areas of our lives. The next time you change your baby's diaper, chop a carrot, embrace your partner as he or she returns home, carry the garbage out, put your shoes on, ask: "Can I make it lighter?" This question awakens that part of us that smiles as butterflies alight in front of us, as leaves dance in the wind. In time we may sense how all life is a t'ai chi dance—and that all the beings of this world, even the tiniest ant, are our dancing partners.

Completion

Completion is actually a movement that I added several years ago because I wished to end the form in the same way in which it begins. In fact, it is nothing more than what one would do if, having finished the form, one wanted immediately to begin again. So the ending is also the beginning, in the true t'ai chi spirit.

To begin, you are standing with your feet parallel and shoulder-width apart. The hands are hanging at your sides, with a space under each arm the size of your own fist and the palms facing backward. This is exactly the same position as at the end of Preparation.

Then draw your left foot to your right one so that the heels are touching and the feet are forming a V-shape. At the same time, turn the hands so that the palms are facing the body. Remember to keep a space under your arms.

At this point I always bow forward slightly. It is also possible to bring the palms together and bow at the waist, if that is comfortable for you. The bow is a way for me to acknowledge the gratitude that I feel at the end of the form. It arose spontaneously one day and I kept it because it seems to gather all the threads of my life and make them present in one gesture.

If a bow is not your way of expressing such a moment, then I invite you to find your own way of ending the form. Whatever gesture or movement you create, think of it as a deeply personal way of acknowledging your own journey, not only through the form, but in the form that is your life.

28

Waiting at the Entrance—Again

In the mid-1980s a friend of mine told me about a European teacher of Asian martial arts who had the ability to repel any attack through mental force alone. At the time, he lived in seclusion with his students and family in the countryside. My friend, who was an external student of the teacher, arranged for me to go for a five-day visit.

When I arrived late one evening, I was greeted at the door by a member of the community. She took me across the street to a local farmhouse that rented rooms to occasional visitors like me. I was told to return to the center at nine o'clock sharp the next morning.

Promptly at 9:00 A.M. I was shown into a large room that served as the dining and communal room. The same woman from the night before told me to take a seat at a corner table. There I was to wait until I was called to meet the teacher. She told me not to leave the room unless I needed to go to the toilet. Looking at my briefcase, she asked if I had some work to keep me busy. Yes, I assured her, I had plenty to do. She nodded approvingly, then left quickly.

Several hours went by. Occasionally members of the community walked through the room. Aside from brief moments of eye contact, there was no other exchange between us. I assumed that they were being silent as part of their rules of training, so I did not attempt to engage anyone in conversation.

At noon at least twenty-five people filed into the room where I sat. No one joined me at my small table. People smiled politely but no one talked to me. Meals were eaten in silence, with men and women sitting separately.

I knew that I was being tested in a classical Asian way. In olden times, students were never admitted immediately to see the teacher or into the monastery or training hall. In some Japanese Zen traditions even today, a student must sit in zazen for five days at the entrance to the temple before being admitted to train. I was proud to be following this example. And I was a bit smug that I saw through everything. I was determined to appear worthy enough to be allowed admittance. This pride and determination were to be worn to the bone over the next few days.

I sat at the corner table for five days. The day's rhythm was always the same. I would be ushered in at 9:00 A.M. and shown out at 9:00 P.M. to go to bed. After lunch I was told to rest in my room and return at 3:00 P.M. The guest master was the only person who talked to me in those five days—and then only when I asked a question or she needed to tell me something.

The second day passed in the same fashion as the first. I held on to my smugness as best I could, but at times, despite my best efforts to suppress them, I felt twinges of anger and impatience. I neutralized them immediately by telling my-self, "Come on, you know the score. Just play the game!" As the day wore on, it became more difficult to concentrate, and I began to feel as I do when taking a long flight. I stood and stretched many times, made frequent trips to the toilet, or got caught up in daydreaming. I fell into bed that night wondering what the hell I was doing there anyway.

On the third day my anger rose to the surface. I still had enough control to keep my mouth shut, but my actions were short, choppy, and aggressive. I was pissed off about everything: the chair, the room, the food, the people, the air I breathed. I must have stared quite angrily at people during lunch, because now they completely ignored me. When they left after lunch, I felt as if I were being abandoned on a desert island and condemned to aloneness forever.

That evening there was a change in routine. Board games and cards were pulled out, and people began talking. At some point the teacher arrived—my first opportunity to observe him. His exuberant manner matched his physical presence: a sense of massiveness, boundless energy, and penetrating eyes. I was invited to join in. I knew, without being told, that I should not ask questions. Just play the game! It was clear that this recreation period was as much a part of the training as anything else they did.

On the fourth day I felt completely drained. Several times during the day I cried quietly. I didn't feel anything anymore, not pride, anger, or impatience. I had neither the energy to work productively nor the energy to get up and leave. I had lost all hope. I went to bed that evening feeling that I had failed completely.

I woke the morning of the fifth day knowing it was my last day. I entered the communal room, went to my usual place, pulled out my books, and began working. I didn't expect anything in particular and had stopped trying to figure things out. I simply got on with my work, ate lunch with the others, returned to work afterward. The day went quickly, and I felt focused and centered. I got a lot done that day.

After dinner the guest master asked me to follow her. We entered a large training hall and crossed over to a small, dim office, lit only by candlelight. The teacher was waiting for me in his chair.

He looked at me for a long time, his eyes laughing, and said in a light tone, "You looked a bit nervous when you arrived. I thought you needed some time to settle down." That was all he said in reference to the five days I had sat waiting in the communal room.

"How did you know I would go along with it?" I asked.

"Because everyone does," he said jovially. "But few people make it through the five days."

"Does it mean I'm special?" I asked, half joking, half hoping.

"Special? No. Just greedy. Very greedy!"

We talked long into the night. Because of language difficulties, I understood only a portion of what he said. But much more happened that night that went beyond words. Though I never formally became his student, I count him as one of my teachers. He taught me to accept my greed and hunger and to see that they can be transformed into clear intention, motivation, and a capacity to focus. His energy and dedication had created a place where I could wait and, in doing so, really go to the end of hope.

Why is it so important to give up hope? Hope in itself is not the problem. But the expectations and projections, the secret dreams that often accompany hope, can actually sabotage our chance of ever reaching what we have hoped for. Hope can also lead to paralysis because in itself having hope can be very satisfying. As long as we are focused on some future pleasant event, we don't really have to be present in the here and now, or take care of things that come up or that we mess up.

There are many times in studying t'ai chi that it can feel like waiting at the entrance. The promise of the fruits of practice—experiencing peace of mind and improved coordination, defeating people in push hands—all seem to be just on the other side of the door. The longer we have to wait, the more our frustration rises.

Waiting at the entrance is really about staying power, about perseverance, and about facing the demons that come up and want to distract us. In fact, the waiting provokes impatience. It pushes our buttons. If we really go the distance, though, we will see how all our mechanisms for trying to master the situation are eventually exhausted. Then we will be free of their weight—and free to act.

No one gives up hope voluntarily. But because we are so tenacious in holding on, we sometimes have to be tricked into situations where we are overwhelmed. Letting go usually happens when we are exhausted, physically or mentally. When we do let go, which can be nothing more than accepting that we need to practice a move one more time, it feels like a big relief.

Waiting at the entrance is rather like standing in the face of a huge wave. We can frantically try to outswim it, but as every kid at the ocean knows, it is far better to dive directly into the wave just as it crests. We dive through to the calm on the other side of the wave and can watch with joy—and later equanimity—as the wave pounds to the shore.

And then we turn around and wait for the next wave.

29

The End of the Rainbow

Several years ago a woman I had met during a t'ai chi seminar was giving me a ride home. We had been discussing the issue of authenticity in t'ai chi when suddenly the gloriously blue sky filled with dark clouds. A moment later rain poured down heavily. In the magical way that sometimes happens, the sun came out and highlighted the mass of rain-filled clouds from behind. "This is just the kind of weather for rainbows," I said, looking around. "Maybe we'll see one."

"Do you know where the rainbow begins?" my companion asked dreamily.

"No," I said hesitantly, wondering at how her tone had changed completely from the rather dry discussion we had been having.

"Well, I never did either. But one day something happened to me that showed me where rainbows begin. Would you like to hear the story?"

"Yes," I answered happily.

"I was riding in a car driven by a friend. The weather was very much like today's. I was going through a difficult time in my life. My husband had just suffered a massive heart attack. We were not sure he would make it. And even if he did, he would probably never be able to work again. I didn't know how we would survive financially. I was full of worry.

"Suddenly it began to rain, just like now. And then the sun came out. I didn't notice much of anything because I was so wrapped up in my own thoughts. But then I became aware of a feeling of warmth. I looked down and saw that one end of the rainbow was in my lap.

"We drove along like that for a few minutes. At first I said nothing, but then I told my friend and she glanced over.

" 'Do you see it?' I asked.

" 'Oh, my God! It's true!' she said.

"I closed my eyes and sat with the end of the rainbow in my lap. We instinctively remained silent. The warmth spread throughout my body, and I felt a sense of well-being I had not experienced since I was a child. When I opened my eyes a few minutes later, the rainbow was gone.

"I told my husband what had happened when I got home. He just laughed at me and asked how much wine I had at lunch. But I insisted that it happened. He thought about it for a while and later announced that the whole thing was just an optical illusion. The rainbow had probably been reflected through the glass in such a way that it seemed to begin in my lap.

" 'In any case, I don't see any pot of gold around here, do you?' he said, and with that the discussion was over.

"I can't tell you why," she continued, "but that experience changed my life. From that day on, I stopped feeling that we had suffered a blow of fate. Although we had to change so many things and make difficult decisions, I no longer felt a victim. I knew that if I stopped running away from the problems and faced them, we would make it. Maybe not in the style we were accustomed to. But I was willing to live with the change. It was almost as if I had come through a period of mourning and was now ready to gather that energy and put it into my life.

"It doesn't matter whether the rainbow was really in my lap. I only know that whatever happened, I found a place deep inside myself where I could face things, one thing at a time. I found my way home—to myself. That is the only kind of authenticity I care about."

There is a part of the t'ai chi community, as in other martial arts and the world at large, that lays a great deal of emphasis on things being "authentic." Some t'ai chi schools and teachers say they are teaching the "authentic" or "original" form of a particular tradition, which implies that anything else is, at the worst, a fake, and at the least, not as good.

There are cultural reasons for linking a t'ai chi form to illustrious founders, which include a concern for honoring ancestors, a desire to maintain a sense of a continuous present (that the past is alive in the present), and a wish to preserve a legacy, which t'ai chi forms are considered to be. There are economic reasons for doing this, including the fact that anything with the title "authentic" or "original" tends to sell well. In the t'ai chi world, as in any other world, market forces and competition lead some teachers and schools to engage in age-old but not necessarily skillful promotion techniques. And there are political reasons to insist on being the source and arbiter of a tradition, which enhances the status of a nation that is the birthplace of an art.

There are also psychological reasons for authenticity having such a strong attraction. Believing that you belong to an authentic tradition may sometimes be a strong motivator because it helps give an external sense of worth to one's practice. Everybody likes a winner, so to speak. A carefully nurtured tradition in which the legacy of the past is preserved can also communicate something of great value: when we learn something from that school, we are partaking in a cultural treasure.

There are many uses of the past, but it is not my aim here to get into the pros and cons of such cultural mechanisms. But as far as t'ai chi practice is concerned, it can be very helpful, indeed necessary, that we confront the issue of authenticity. Because if we do it skillfully, it pushes us to explore the essence of t'ai chi.

My trip to Taiwan in 1986 was a real eye-opener in this respect. Among other things, I wanted to study push hands with the teacher of an acquaintance of mine. When Marlies, my traveling companion, and I arrived at the master's school, we were invited to join the t'ai chi form class. Although it was not my interest to learn this teacher's form, I knew it would be extremely rude to refuse the invitation.

Up to that point I had studied only with my own teachers and had not seen much of other styles close-up. When I began studying this new form, it seemed so different. Whereas I was used to doing many of the moves with my weight on the forward leg, including pushing, most of their movements were done with the weight on the back leg. It was a completely new experience to do moves like Fair Lady or Push this way. The biggest problem, however, was not the physical execution but the rebellion that was going on in my mind.

I remember at one point saying to myself, "This is not t'ai chi. I don't know what they're doing, but this can't be right." I was subtle enough to keep my thoughts to myself, but my ideas were interfering with my practice. The fact was that I spent so much time protesting in my mind that I could hardly remember any moves, although we studied the form at least three times a week.

After the morning class each day, we stayed behind for a small private class in the t'ai chi fan form developed by this master, taught by one of his students. The fan form, in which the fan can be used as a weapon, was new for me, and I was enjoying the experience immensely. It incorporated the same kind of footwork as in the solo form, but somehow I had no problem with it at all. This situation continued for some weeks.

One evening as we were learning a move in the weaponless t'ai chi form, I was very tired. I followed the master as if I were on automatic pilot. When we came to the movement Push, I just flowed through the move smoothly, without my usual mental protest. At that moment something dropped in my mind. For the rest of the evening the class went fine. For the first time, the form felt natural.

As I walked down the mountain the next morning to catch a 5:00 A.M. bus, my mind was quiet. The cool air was fresh, and the predawn light slowly filled the sky. The road to the bus stop wound among the steep hills and cliffs of the national park where we were staying in a guest house. Suddenly from the cliff above me, a cry pierced the air and it shivered through my whole body.

Someone was obviously practicing chi kung, emitting one of the six healing tones. Tears filled my eyes and I felt a deep link to that person—and to all the people who were practicing throughout the park. We were all doing different styles and forms, but in that moment, I knew we were one body.

The t'ai chi principles can be expressed in ways that may appear different at first, but if you go beyond appearances, you will be able to discover the source of the principles in all their variations. If the principles are truly embodied in the form, we can appreciate various nuances while remaining firmly rooted and at home in our own. The spirit of authenticity has nothing to do with belonging to the right tradition, though it can sometimes look like that. Go beyond appearances or statements that others make and look into the heart of what you see. It is a challenge to see beyond differences to the principles that unite all the forms. But when you do, you'll know indeed where the end of the rainbow begins.

30

Beginning Again

Whenever I teach the last movement of a t'ai chi form, I never tell my students we are at the end. Normally I would demonstrate each new movement, but when it is the last one, I tell the group we are doing an exercise in observation and that they should just follow me. Sometimes one person realizes what is going on and, as if a conspirator, continues to play along in silence, perhaps exchanging a knowing smile with me. But for most students, it takes a few moments of standing in silence at the end of the form before they catch on. And then the group erupts.

"I don't believe it!" says one. "I thought the form was much longer!" says another. Another says in surprise, "We did it . . . I did it!" And the comments continue, the content depending on each person's story and perspective on the form.

After a few minutes I call the group back together and we begin studying the last movement in depth. We work on it the same way we have on all the others. It's not special anymore. And that's as it should be.

I always leave enough time when teaching the last movement so that we can return to a normal class atmosphere following the exchange of remarks and congratulations. I consider this return to practice essential. In doing so, I want to send a message to my students that I hope will influence their future relationship to t'ai chi. That message is: No matter where we are in our training, whether advanced or just finishing the form, true practice is imbued with the spirit of beginning again. That spirit can be characterized by different shades—excitement, curiosity, boredom, frustration, determination, perfectionism, joy—but deep down there is faith in the knowledge that growth occurs only when we are willing to go back into what we know and do it again.

Why is this so important? There is an interesting statistic that shows the problem that develops when we don't have the spirit of beginning again. It was included in a survey of martial arts students that asked, among other questions, at what point they stopped training regularly. As would be expected, a large number quit within the first year. But a second big exodus is when students receive the equivalent of the black belt.

In many martial arts traditions, the training period leading up to the black belt test or its equivalent is highly structured, and the curriculum is straightforward. The various lower belt tests in between give motivation at crucial points along the way, as well as a sense of steadily progressing toward a goal. Students do their period of most intensive training in the six months or so leading up to the test. I know people who have attended class almost every evening for months prior to their tests. I have heard of others who have taken a leave of absence from their jobs so they could train more. More than one relationship has been strained by the tension created when one partner is so focused on his or her upcoming exam.

The black belt exam is a big occasion. Often the whole school turns out for it, and sometimes visiting dignitaries, other martial arts masters, and/or friends of the teacher are present. The exam is a ritual and an opportunity for all those involved in this art to bear witness to the student's effort and to that of his teacher and partners, to honor the lineage, and to honor the martial art as a whole. All eyes are on the black belt candidate. The opponents who challenge the candidate are determined not only to give him a run for his money but to look good.

Being awarded the black belt produces tremendous exhilaration—and then a big letdown. Everything that comes after is anticlimactic. There seems to be nothing more to train for, nothing to attain.

Quitting is just one result that may follow a period of intense exertion. A sense of emptiness, depression, frustration, losing one's bearings, and boredom, among other things, can appear after we have reached either an external or a self-defined goal. It can happen after events as varied as the black belt exam, an intensive meditation retreat, a wedding, giving birth, sailing single-handed around the world, being a member of the all-women's team to walk to the Arctic, getting a bachelor of arts degree, or making a new scientific discovery. Those moments when we close the door behind us, when there are no more deadlines, rituals, or tasks to accomplish, can leave us feeling as if we'd fallen into a vast hole.

There are two main ways of working with this situation. We can stay at the bottom of the hole and get accustomed to life there. Or we can raise our eyes even slightly and notice that there are some niches in the wall that we can use as handles. The moment we reach for that first handle is the same moment we begin practicing again after we finish learning the form. And while it's a good start, it's not enough. We have to reach for the next handle; we have to go over a move one more time . . . and another and another.

There are certainly all sorts of reasons, psychological and biological, why periods of depression follow times of intense exertion. These times can sometimes be so difficult to handle that they go beyond our personal resources and require that we seek help: medical care, psychological counseling, self-help groups are some possibilities. But the light at the end of the tunnel always opens to the same place: a path that requires that we set one foot after the other, to continuously begin again.

One tendency we have when we finish learning the form is to want to freeze it. Then each time we do t'ai chi, we simply repeat what we know. While it's known to us, it's comfortable. Beginning again, however, asks us to risk what we know, to open ourselves to going deeper by challenging, pulling apart, and questioning, "What is it that I really learned? And have I really learned it?"

This is exactly the way we work in the second year of my t'ai chi intensive training program. I call the second-year series Deepening the Form. In the first meeting, I explain that we are going to start at the beginning again. We will examine, play with, and pull apart the t'ai chi form that they have just learned. In the first year we focused on the outward shape of the movements. Now we will play with the form from the inside out.

One of the things I might do with a group during this year is an exercise in which I ask them to experience their mind flowing through their body—into their arms and down to their hands—as they do the form. To prepare them for this, we do an exercise called Energy Extension.

There is often a noticeable change in a student's form after doing Energy Extension. Not only do the hands become more alive but the whole posture can change. We even have a name for the expression of the hands: it's called Beautiful Lady's Hand. (Wolfe Lowenthal's book *There Are No Secrets* has a picture of Professor Cheng Man-ching's hand on the cover, which expresses this principle: soft yet clearly shaped, full of energy that is flowing and extending.) The change is usually not permanent, as old ways die hard, but for that shining moment, the student experiences a possibility of how his form can tingle.

Many students experience a low point during the first weekend of the second-year workshop series. The thrill of finishing the form is gone in the summer wind. Now it feels like hard work again.

Sometime during the weekend I always say, "Now you know what it means to be an advanced student." Invariably a chorus of groans, sighs, or curses follows. Some students look at me with weary eyes; some shoot me looks that could topple hundred-foot trees. But then we sit down with a cup of tea and talk about what is coming up. These times of sharing are important. Each student hears that he or she is not alone in feeling disappointment, frustration, or tiredness. Students see that they are not unique, that everyone is indeed participating in the same process. Each person is going through what all t'ai chi students, their teachers, and their teachers' teachers have gone through before them.

The t'ai chi form ends in the standing posture with which we begin the form. If we choose to, we could do the form again, and again and again. Each time, we have the opportunity to look, to open, and to feel. There is truly a miracle—and a wealth of wisdom—in that one small moment of beginning at the beginning of the beginning.

31

Wholeheartedness

One of the challenges I present my students after they have learned the form is to work it out in the opposite direction by themselves. In practice it means that where you turned left before, you now turn right; if you stepped forward with the right foot, now you step forward with the left.

I remember one occasion many years ago when I presented a group with a particularly difficult version of this exercise. Perhaps I was inspired by the fact that the whole group was very committed to t'ai chi and practiced intensively. Their spirit had encouraged me to set up a teacher-training program in order to provide a forum in which they could continue to be challenged. In any case, the exercise was to be quite a learning experience for all of us.

We had gone away for the weekend in order to have time to live, breathe, and eat t'ai chi for two and a half days. On the afternoon of the second day, I told the group I wanted to give them a big puzzle. The only rule was that each person had to work on his or her own and not talk to the others for as long as the exercise lasted.

I then asked each of them to figure out how to do the first half of the form in the other direction. Their goal should be to reach the end of the first half, but the most important thing was to work systematically and get as far as they could. "Any time you feel like turning to your neighbor and asking, 'How does this part go?' turn the question back onto yourself. The answer is in your own form. You've just got to find it."

First each person worked out the best way to tackle the exercise. Most noticed almost immediately their automatic tendency to turn in the accustomed direction. It was almost as if the body had a mind and will of its own. Time and again someone would turn to the right, only to break off the movement and start again. After a number of tries it ran more smoothly. But if the concentration faded for even a moment, it was easy to shift to automatic pilot.

Learning the form to the left mirrors exactly how we learn the form to the right. First we have to become familiar with the shape of the movement, then practice it, then run the form back a few movements to make sure that the transition between the previous move and the next one is seamless.

Most of the students figured out that the best way to learn the movements to the left was to first practice them to the right. Then it became a process of transposing from right to left. Just as when we transpose music to a different key, all the elements are there but in a new context. Music transposed just one key can sound completely different, yet the old melody is right there within it.

For two hours they seesawed through the form. First to the right, then to the left, then back again. Each student had his own pace, and soon they were all at different stages in the form. Some movements were more difficult than others, such as Single Whip, but the method of dealing with each was always the same. Right, left, right . . . and back again.

Still waters run deep, they say, but these waters were

sometimes churning. More than once I thought a student would come over to me and express her frustration, but the exercise was a strong enough container to hold it all. Some people were working so hard that sweat dripped down their faces—and it was not a particularly warm day. Often people sat or lay down for a few moments, obviously exhausted. One person broke down and cried quietly.

As I sat in the corner and watched, it was difficult for me not to intervene. I was moved by their efforts, but especially by the person who cried openly. I knew she was facing difficulties in her private life, and the exercise was obviously pushing those buttons. But if I intervened, I would be robbing her of the chance to keep trying. Here, in this relatively safe space, there were lessons to be learned—lessons that could be applied to daily life.

After two hours I called the exercise to a halt. Some people had gone beyond the first half; others were not yet there but close. It was time for dinner, and we agreed that we would not talk about our experience but save everything for after our evening meeting.

It was a night of magic, one of the most profound sharings I have ever participated in. We sat down in a room filled with candlelight and kept silent for some time as we settled in. I then asked a question, inviting each person to answer when and if he or she wanted to. The only rule was not to engage in discussion but to take turns speaking. My question was short: "What is t'ai chi?"

It became clear that the content of the exercise was much more than simply doing the form to the left. It was a challenge and an invitation to the heart. The most important thing, one woman explained, was being able to accept herself where she was. Before she was really able to do that, her own self-judgments and recriminations got in the way and prevented her from making her best effort.

Others expressed similar sentiments. Our discussion went on for hours, periods of silence filling the space between speakers. As the candles burned down and the wee hours of the night approached, we joined hands and stood for a long period in silence. A few hours later we would be sitting together in dawn zazen, a seamless transition from movement to stillness.

Later, in reflecting on that day and the evening's sharing, I came to understand the heart of what was going on. And it was really a matter of the heart. In fact, the most powerful invitation of that exercise was the opportunity to express wholeheartedness. It was a chance to practice with the whole heart, an opportunity that many of us shy away from because of fear.

The fear of putting our whole heart into something is based on the fear of breaking our heart. Thus we are often threatened by the idea of making a commitment to something, most of all to ourselves. We shy away from activities that emphasize effort, calling discipline a practice of extremists. We excuse ourselves by saying, "I only want to learn a bit of t'ai chi; I don't want to begin a spiritual practice" or "I just came here to deal with my back pain; as long as t'ai chi can help me with that, that's all I'm interested in."

There are many reasons why people begin t'ai chi, but few stay with it for long if they don't find some way of putting their heart into it. Of course, that may express itself very differently for each person. For someone to carve out twenty minutes in her day to practice may be as difficult as for someone else to train two hours per day. Wholeheartedness is not something measured in terms of time or amount but in terms of the willingness to work with everything that comes up as part of the learning experience, including resistance to facing ourselves. Pema Chödrön writes in *The Wisdom of No Escape* what an invitation to express wholeheartedness can mean:

Wholeheartedness is a precious gift, but no one can actually give it to you. You have to find the path that has heart and then walk it impeccably. In doing that, you again and again encounter your own uptightness, your own headaches, your own falling flat on your face. But in wholeheartedly practicing and wholeheartedly following that path, this inconvenience is not an obstacle. It's simply a certain texture of life, a certain energy of life. Not only that, sometimes when you just get flying and it all feels so good and you think, "This is it, this is the path that has heart," you suddenly fall flat on your face. Everybody's looking at you. You say to yourself, "What happened to that path that had heart? This feels like the path of mud in the face." Since you are wholeheartedly committed to the warrior's journey, it pricks you, it pokes you. It's like someone laughing in your ear, challenging you to figure out what to do when you don't know what to do. It humbles you. It opens your heart.[1]

32

Let Your T'ai Chi Sing

A woman I know decided to visit a coach because she felt blocked in her work. Margaret was a teacher who had just finished training in a method that she hoped to introduce in the area where she lived. Her plans included approaching businesses as well as medical and health professionals to see if they were interested in the program. Developing this circle of prospective clients meant she would be running with a whole different crowd of people from those she normally worked with. She was nearing fifty, feeling rundown and afraid of failing. She knew that her old ways of working would have to be revamped and re-created for this new client group. She was scared, and no amount of confidence boosting or pep talks from her husband and friends could convince her she had what it took to be successful.

During the first session, Margaret mainly talked and the coach listened. When she returned for the next visit, Margaret was ready to sit down with pencil and paper and get to work. She was not prepared for the coach's question.

"What is the thing that gives you the most joy?" the coach asked.

Margaret thought about it for a moment. "Working with others," she said.

"Bullshit!" said the coach. "Speak from the heart."

Margaret was taken aback. What has this got to do with my problem? she wondered. But she decided to take the question seriously and thought for a moment. She had a flash of something.

"Singing. I love to sing," Margaret said quietly. She felt naked, completely exposed.

"Well, sing!" said the coach

"What, right here, now?"

"Yes! Do what you most love to do. Right now."

Margaret couldn't believe this was happening. Her first impulse was to hem and haw. "I can't do it right here. I'm not prepared. This isn't the right environment."

The coach just sat patiently and waited. By this point Margaret was pacing the floor in front of her. What she had said and what she was feeling didn't match at all. In fact, a spark of desire was being fanned in her. Someone had just asked her to sing! In the shower and when she was alone in a big room were the only places she sang these days. Those days of belting out a song in the junior high school chorus or in her friend's living room, where she memorized the scores of ten musicals from overture to curtain call, were thirty-five long years ago. And yet the invitation to sing was tingling her bones.

Someone inside her made the decision. She turned to the coach, stood wide, and took a deep breath. And she began to sing.

At first Margaret was barely audible. Her voice shook and she thought she would have to stop. But each phrase seemed to build on the next, and the song sang itself. By the time she reached the crescendo, the whole room was filled with her voice. Her arms outstretched, she was reaching for the heights of the song with a part of her that was like a bird that had been released from its tether to soar through the wide sky.

Tears were streaming down the coach's face, and Margaret accepted each one in deep appreciation. Only later, in the vast quiet that filled the room, did she realize she had unconsciously chosen to sing "Climb Every Mountain" from *The Sound of Music*. If she had thought about it for weeks, she couldn't have picked a more appropriate song. She knew that this was the song and these were words that were singing all the time in her soul. But she hadn't been listening.

I know this well. Because Margaret is me.

Deep in this story is a very important lesson about our relationship to t'ai chi. The form offers a measure of security, regularity, and certainty within an uncertain world: we learn something that is prescribed and consistent—always done in the same way. Many of my students say that the thing they most value about their t'ai chi class is that it feels like the eye of the storm—a period of calmness and silence each week in the middle of the raging storm of life. It is so reassuring and calming not to be surprised all the time. Even when confronted with having to learn a new movement, they know it will soon enter their repertoire and feel trusted and trustworthy.

However, we can get stuck in not wanting to rock the boat. There is a tendency in t'ai chi, as in many other things, to try to freeze the form in the name of preserving tradition. This is especially true of forms and practices that are brought from one culture and introduced into another. What often begins with good intentions goes beyond preservation to become more like embalming. Whether out of fear of making a mistake, lack of trust in one's own capacity, or the need to maintain authority, some t'ai chi practitioners and teachers resist innovation with all their might. Innovation is blasphemy, the sacred is made profane.

Jalaja Bonheim writes in her book *The Serpent and the Wave: A Guide to Movement Meditation* that a form "can be a tool for enlightenment, but it can also be a repressive device, stifling individuality and expressiveness."[1] This is as true of the t'ai chi form as it is of anything else. The moment we freeze the form, the moment we lose the tension between precision and spontaneity, we have created a prison, a dead ritual, a nailed-down coffin.

There are many examples in traditions both East and West where innovation is valued, but sometimes the innovation can be very subtle. For example, in Noh, one of the most highly ritualized Japanese theater forms, a performer's role and repertoire of movements are based on centuries-old defined rules. The way each character moves on the stage is strictly traditional and must be learned like a form. Everything is done exactly the same way it has been done for hundreds of years.

One would think that in such a rigid world, innovation would be frowned upon. On a large scale that is definitely true. But minute changes do take place from time to time. In fact, a great performer is recognized by his skill in suggesting the most subtle change. It may be as small as changing the number of steps needed to cross the stage or looking to the left instead of looking to the right. I've been told that Noh aficionados sit on the edge of their seats, holding their breath, as an actor executes an innovation. It is a very special moment. For, what is in that moment an innovation could become part of the tradition and be taught as part of the form for decades to come.

If we are not willing to risk playing with our form, we are in danger of becoming buried alive within it. I consider that the highest t'ai chi skill is to play with the form. Flowing between form and no form is the mark of a great t'ai chi practitioner. Playing with the form can mean doing it at different speeds or with various kinds of steps (wide or narrow). Like kung fu practitioners, we can even pretend we are drunk or old or very young. One thing I like to do with my classes is to put on some really hot, throbbing soul music and announce that the t'ai chi disco is open. Or we do a kind of medley of t'ai chi with classical, New Age, jazz, and reggae music all flowing through our form.

After finishing such a playful period with your form, it is important to do it at least once in the way that you usually do it. Begin again, this time with the precision and careful attention to detail that you have practiced for months or years. You may sense that even your very familiar form has shifted just a bit. It may feel more spacious, the shapes rounder; there may be a lighter and more balanced feel to the movements. Experience these moments as they are, but don't try to hold on to them either. The effect is rather like trying to find one's balance by shifting from one position to another. Somewhere in the shift is the moment of perfect balance. It can only really be experienced in the midst of movement, just as we experience the expanse of our life not in isolated moments but in the ebb and flow of existence.

In the beginning it can be disconcerting to break out of our accustomed form, but the secret is in letting go of the need to be perfect. In sacrificing and risking one's accomplishment, in surrendering to the music, one discovers a whole new idea of center. The center is not fixed but can be experienced in each moment, whether one is moving wildly or with deliberation. In that place of calm and centeredness, the form flows out of us and melts into the shape of the music. It is liberating and liberated, exotic and familiar, spare and luxuriant. It may feel like abandonment, but the only thing you are giving up is familiarity.

Open your arms, take a wide stance, and let your t'ai chi sing. Let it dance you. Let it be.

AFTERWORD

*O*ne does not have to be a great soul to make a commitment to put one's body and soul into practicing t'ai chi. In welcoming obstacles or our own mistakes as opportunities to learn, we make the deepest commitment to t'ai chi and ourselves that is possible. Even as we establish a regular practice rhythm, doubts and distractions continually come up. By acknowledging our resistances as obstacles to explore, we stop forcing ourselves to Do something! and work more gently with what's there. We don't rise to the challenge by pumping ourselves up with verbal encouragement or forced affirmations. We go on, hearing but not heeding our doubts, building a foundation of trust and quiet determination based on experience. More than anything else, we learn to trust the wisdom of the body in practicing t'ai chi. When the body has a chance simply to weave its magic, to feel its knowledge, then we experience confidence and a sense of joy in practice, whether we are a beginner or a master.

APPENDIX

Getting Started or Starting Again

In the pages that follow I answer some of the most frequently asked questions about establishing and maintaining a t'ai chi practice. The suggestions I make are meant to be guidelines, not rules. They are appropriate both for the beginning student and for more experienced students who are looking for ways to invigorate their training. Each practitioner will discover for herself over time what is helpful and what just takes up time or is unskillful. If there is any measure of success to our practice, then it is to the degree that it subtly infuses our life and spirit in a way that awakens our curiosity and a quiet determination to look, listen, and open our eyes to the world around us and to ourselves.

Establishing a regular t'ai chi practice is really a question of finding the proper balance. Some people begin with such rigid requirements that it is almost impossible to follow through on them. Others have a very laid-back attitude and say they will practice when they feel like it. If the goal is to develop and deepen one's experience of t'ai chi, neither of these paths will be very successful.

What generally seems to work best is first to experiment within one's life to find the appropriate practice mode. Finding the right place, time of day, way, and amount of time to practice, all may require some experimentation. But once you find something that seems to work, stick to it. Then your practice mode becomes like a raft. In the quiet waters of your life you float along, enjoying the scenery and becoming more and more familiar with it. When you hit the rapids of your life, you know the craft of rafting intimately and can steer through the most turbulent waters.

How Much Should I Practice?

The first question that usually pops up about how to practice is How much? "Do I need to practice every day? How much is enough? What happens if I miss a day?"

We all know the answer to the question of how much to practice: how much you get out of something depends on how much you put into it. If you practice an hour a day, it shows. If you practice ten minutes a day, it shows. And if you don't practice at all, it shows.

We really don't want to hear this though. We'd much rather believe that we can practice a little and somehow our progress will show in exponential amounts. Even more, we'd like to believe that just taking part in class is enough and somehow we will magically absorb the skill of a t'ai chi master and manifest it instantly.

Much of what is written in t'ai chi literature or in advertising blurbs doesn't help to change this expectation. Whether the reason is to not scare away potential students or because the teacher learned this way herself, people often write that just fifteen minutes a day is sufficient practice time. Of course, any activity done mindfully is beneficial, but there's no getting around the fact that thirty minutes of mindful activity is better than fifteen minutes.

It really makes no sense for me to prescribe how much someone should practice. The most helpful advice I can give is this: Be realistic. Take several things into consideration. How much can you reasonably set aside each day, given your work, study, or relationship commitments? Once you have decided, then stick to your decision and begin immediately. There are other things you can do to keep yourself on target about practicing. Here are a few suggestions:

- Keep a training journal.
- Enter your workouts on a large calendar that you keep in full view.
- Find someone to train with regularly.
- If you find your practice is flagging, attend extra classes until you feel you are back on track.
- Develop your own prepractice rituals to ease the transition from everyday life to training time (I used to clean house).
- Go out to breakfast or for an early morning walk or jog and come back to a quiet house after everyone has left for work or school.
- Listen to music while warming up.
- Practice sitting meditation before training.
- Find a practice space outdoors and let the walk to it settle you down.
- Go on retreat to a quiet place, away from distraction, where you can schedule your day exactly the way you want.
- Sign up for a t'ai chi workshop or summer camp, where you have the chance to practice for several hours a day and to meet new t'ai chi friends.

Don't try to fit yourself to someone else's ideal of how you should practice. But do try hard to find out what works best for you. It's probably best not to talk too much with others about how you practice. Most people find it difficult to be supportive; we've all learned too well how to be critical. So until you feel centered about what you do, put your energy into yourself rather than into convincing someone else. Generally when we are trying hard to sway someone, we really need to hear ourselves talk positively because we're insecure. If that's the case, look at that, not away. Just practice!

How Should I Practice?

Repeating the form each day so that it becomes a daily routine, like brushing one's teeth or applying body lotion, is a great way of establishing a strong practice. But to deepen our understanding of the form, our training needs to mature. To mature means that we are not satisfied with just a touch-all-the-bases or once-over-lightly training session but that we are willing to go deeply and repeatedly into the movements. In fact, after repeating the form once or twice, we should take a section, or even one move, and work through it very slowly, again and again.

It is sometimes helpful to practice in front of a mirror. It takes time to be able to feel whether we are standing correctly or not. Looking in the mirror is a good way of checking our posture.

It can also be a great motivator. Try looking yourself in the eyes and even talking to yourself when you train in front of the mirror. It can really boost your training spirit. But don't get too attached to your image. Too much focus on the outer form of t'ai chi can end in a kind of Narcissus-like dependency. We must tend to the inner form and sense of t'ai chi and balance it with how it is expressed externally.

Then there is the question of whether or not to practice with music. Like everything else, it should be done in moderation, if at all. Sometimes putting on some soothing, meditative music can help to create an atmosphere that encourages us to train. The music quiets us down and fills the space so that it does not feel so empty.

If you know a form well, it can be great fun to put on music with a strong beat, Latin or reggae music, for example, and just dance the form. I encourage my students to let the music carry them and to let the movements open up and flow spontaneously. To begin with it might feel strange, and you may lose your place. If you have been practicing for a time and the form sits well, then it will feel less like you are doing something completely different than that you are stretching the boundaries of what you know.

I would not suggest playing music for an entire practice session, however. Music tends to set the pace and also encourages us to keep going and keep flowing, but it doesn't encourage us to stop and go back over a move or to be patient if we have stalled in the middle of the form. When you wish to work precisely, it's better to turn the music off.

My chi kung teacher used to tell us that whenever we learned something, we should practice that exclusively for one hundred days. In Chinese culture this number is usually interpreted metaphorically to mean a long time, but it can also be interpreted literally. For example, I had a friend who learned an exercise and was told to practice it for one hundred days. It was not a long sequence, and so she repeated it several times during each training session. At the end of one hundred days, she was given the next sequence and told to practice that for another hundred days. This went on for several years, and when I saw her again it was obvious the training had been very beneficial: she looked wonderful.

The principle of training at one thing for one hundred days had had a profound impact on her life. She had been suffering from a very hectic work schedule that allowed her no time to relax or to do things that she liked. After she began training in the one-hundred-day method, she had to change her life radically to fit it into her schedule. The first thing she learned was to set priorities, which in this case were her own health and peace of mind. Then she learned to do just one thing at a time, which was very soothing.

My friend said, "I used to be in a very linear mode of operation. I went from one thing to another to another, like racking up points in a never-ending card game. But I learned that it is possible to be in a spiral mode, where I do one thing but go deeper and deeper. It seems like doing less, but it is the most satisfying way of being that I have ever experienced."

How Do I Make Time for Practice?

One of the hardest thing about practicing is setting aside time for ourselves. Even finding five minutes to be alone with ourselves can be a struggle. I know how difficult it is from my own experience; it has never been easy for me to practice at home alone. For many years I thought it was a problem of discipline. I simply wasn't focused enough, I told myself.

As the years went on I saw that the issue was really about spending time with myself. I lacked faith that I could practice alone and do something worthwhile. I associated practice with making progress. But the amount that I achieved was very small from one practice session to another. So, rather than risk disappointment, I just didn't practice. Yet the thought of practicing was on my mind all the time. It became an obsession that I thought I could never satisfy.

I learned to work with commitment one practice session at a time. Each morning I made a vow to train that day. I reviewed my schedule to find the best time. When I couldn't practice at the hour set aside, then I did so at any time before going to bed. Some days that meant practicing at midnight. If I really couldn't practice that day, I didn't make excuses. I just practiced the next day as usual.

I used to tell myself, "I can train only when everything is quiet and I don't feel stressed." Since that was rarely the case, you can imagine how much I trained alone to begin with. Finally it dawned on me that I had things upside down. Instead of needing to be quiet to do t'ai chi, I did the form and became quieter. I then made a vow: to do the form, no matter what was going on in my life, at least once a day.

Keeping my vow was the most important element of my training in the beginning. It was a reminder, responsibility, and motivator that kept me returning to training even when there were so many good reasons to do something else. It gave me the space to think in a different way about the words *discipline* and *perseverance*.

Discipline, I came to see, was not about forcing myself to do something but about continuing to train, despite all the doubts and negative thoughts that my mind seemed to throw up. It meant taking quiet notice of my internal dialogue but not taking it so seriously that I became paralyzed.

Perseverance meant developing a simple, regular, no-frills practice rhythm rather than some elaborate training scheme that was too complicated to implement or even remember. It meant setting priorities that I could meet.

These changes in my ideas about the two cornerstones of training helped me stand firm and continue practicing, even as a part of me was already out the door or wanting to leave and quit training altogether because I was frustrated. I could listen to whatever was coming up, but I saw I had a choice as to whether to act on it or not.

When my students ask what time of day they should practice, my first answer is usually, "The best time to practice is when you practice." It is very helpful to practice at a regular time and to establish a routine about what you do in those sessions. But don't make that the goal in itself. Too often something intervenes, and maybe we have to practice later in the day or not at all. We then tend to judge and overload ourselves with negativity, poisoning our attitude toward future practice sessions. We end up not practicing at all because we couldn't do it our way. If this tends to be your story, then see it clearly for what it is. And then practice.

How Do I Make a Space for Practice?

In many martial arts traditions, the training hall is a sacred space. Bowing rituals or lighting incense highlight its special nature as well as honoring the activity that takes place there. Pictures of the art's founders or teaching lineage often adorn the walls, and students may pay homage to those depicted by bowing or offering incense.

The training hall is a space that cradles personal development. Our training is as much spiritual as physical; we touch the core of our being as well as stretch our muscles or refine technique. When we face a partner in push hands and learn to listen to her energy so that we may follow rather than push her around, we are experiencing the watercourse way: water doesn't push, it flows. When we get stuck at the same part in the form for the tenth time and resolve to begin again, rather than throw up our hands in frustration and walk out, we tap into the natural energy of a seedling as it pushes through the soil until it breaks through above ground. The training hall, as the space that witnesses and sets the scene for such an opportunity, is indeed a wonderful place. The following words were part of Professor Cheng Man-Ch'ing's dedication to his t'ai chi school, which he named the Hall of Happiness:

> Let true affection and happy concourse abide in this hall. Let us here correct our past mistakes and lose preoccupation with self. With the constancy of the planets in their courses or of the dragon in his cloud-wrapped path, let us enter the land of health and ever walk within its bounds. Let us fortify ourselves against weakness and learn to be self-reliant, without even a moment's lapse. Then our resolution will become the very air we breathe, the world we live in; then we will be happy as a fish in crystal waters.[1]

Creating a training space at home is essential to supporting your t'ai chi practice. If you're fortunate to have enough living space to set aside a room for your dojo, then do it. But that room should then be reserved for your training or meditation activity. Don't use it as a guest room. When guests come, give them your bedroom and you sleep in the training hall. In this way you can be assured that the atmosphere is preserved.

If you don't have enough space for a separate training

room, then designate an area in your home and mark it off somehow. Perhaps all you can set aside is a rug. That's fine. Many years ago I knew a woman who lived in a tiny East Village apartment in New York City. There was barely enough space in her kitchen to turn around. Yet she managed to paint a t'ai chi symbol on the floor, between the sink and the fridge, and practiced pa kua, one of the three Taoist internal martial arts, along with t'ai chi and hsing i, for many years in this space. People laugh when I tell them to train sword form with a kitchen knife or chopstick when they don't have enough space to play with the sword. I did it for years in my living room when it was too cold to practice in the park, and it worked fine.

Create an area of focus in your space, or a shrine. In this area place a candle, flowers, incense, and pictures of your teacher and his or her teachers. Or a picture of anyone who inspires you. When you travel, create a portable shrine that you take with you. It's a support as well as a reminder, and a very effective way to raise the spirit of practice in a new environment.

Some people have negative associations about creating shrines in their homes. Anything that suggests religion is suspicious, and the last thing we want to do is answer curious questions from Aunt Emma when she visits. But shrines have important functions. They create a space that supports intensity and focus. They are repositories of the energy generated there through practice and concentration. In a sense our training space is also a shrine to ourselves, where we celebrate our basic capacity to awaken physically and mentally. We commemorate this in the sacred objects and in the rituals and activity taking place there.

Developing a simple ritual, such as lighting incense or

bowing on entering your training space, has a powerful effect on motivation. It sets the tone for the time to follow as well as creating a frame around the time spent there. The time is sacred because we dedicate it to our body/spirit, and to staying awake and aware in the present moment.

How Do I Breathe during T'ai Chi?

Usually sometime during the first class, a student asks, "How should I breathe when doing the form?" My answer is always the same: "Just breathe naturally."

I get various responses to my answer. Usually someone shoots back, "Well, I'm having trouble doing just that. In fact, I feel out of breath sometimes."

Generally we get out of breath because we have been concentrating so hard that we actually hold our breath. This happens not only in t'ai chi but in many activities that require concentration. We need to continually remind ourselves to breathe—and to be in touch with the sensation of breathing. The problem usually clears up in time.

I emphasize natural breathing, which means breathing whenever you need to. I feel it's more important to be aware of the sensations in our body during movement than to keep track of the breath. Paying attention to the body keeps us grounded and focused. If we turn our attention to the breath too early, we add something extra that tends to distract us. Rather than listening to our bodies and sensing them, we tend to control the movements, especially as we try to fit them to our breathing pattern.

Some students who have experience in other martial arts find it difficult to accept my answer. They are used to doing breathing exercises in a controlled manner. They are told to take deep breaths, make sucking noises, puff out their chest, or hold their breath for long periods.

I recently experienced this way of breathing in an introductory Zen workshop led by a Japanese teacher who also happened to be a kendo expert. During a seven-minute period of zazen, he told us to take long deep breaths, putting an emphasis on making the in-breath as deep as possible. Then at the end of the deep-breathing period, he asked three of his own students how many breaths they had taken. We repeated the exercise, this time making the out-breaths as long as possible. At the end of the second period of seven minutes, he asked the same students how many breaths they had taken.

During the first deep-breathing period, I attended to my breath in a relaxed manner, trying to neither deepen nor extend it. I counted about fifty breaths for the seven-minute period, which meant about seven breaths a minute.

During the second period when we concentrated on our out-breaths, I tried to get my score down. I was somewhat embarrassed because the teacher's students had said they breathed three times per minute during the first round. I took very deep breaths and exhaled as slowly as I could. I felt a great deal of pushing and tension in general, but I kept going.

At the end of the second period I noted that I had indeed cut my score in half. But instead of feeling balanced as I did after the first period, I now felt as if I had been in competition with myself. I also felt stressed and mentally agitated. My jaw hurt. If I had continued in this way, should the teacher have ever asked me what my score was, I would probably have answered him through clenched teeth. I don't advocate this kind of training.

The way we train is a mirror for how we conduct our life in general. What kind of face would you like to see reflected back to you when you look in the mirror of life? Should it be healthy, with a relaxed, calm look? Or do you prefer the dark, angry, and tightened face of someone who hands out poisoned apples to all competitors.

How Do I Find a Teacher?

Choosing a teacher very much depends on what you want. Teachers of t'ai chi may emphasize different things: health, martial arts, the aesthetic qualities of the movements, spiritual practice, physical exercise. It is important to choose a teacher whose own direction corresponds with your priorities. If you are interested in t'ai chi as a movement art similar to dance, it makes no sense to choose a teacher who emphasizes t'ai chi as a martial art or whose background is in kick boxing. If you want to study t'ai chi as a martial art, then working with a teacher who has no fighting experience is unrealistic. Of course things can change as time goes on, but in the beginning it is important to find a good match. That's not to say we can't learn something that will help us from any good teacher. But don't force yourself to study with someone just because you think that teacher is good for you. Down deep there has to be a sense that the teacher you decide to study with is someone you can work with, respect, and follow.

Many people think that they have to study with a great master when they first begin t'ai chi. This is not necessary. In fact, it can be less than satisfying. Compare it with studying the piano. Would a beginning piano student really be able to profit from learning from someone like Arthur Rubenstein? And would a great pianist have the time, patience, and willingness to work with a student who first needs to learn the notes, develop flexibility in the fingers, and be able to play Chopin and Beethoven without batting an eyelash?

Look for teachers who you feel are honest in the way they represent themselves, who can answer you clearly when you ask them with whom they have studied. There are many teachers calling themselves masters who are self-appointed and not really at the level where they can embody that title. When in doubt, remember that in the East a teacher never called herself or himself a master. It was always a title awarded to the teacher by peers.

Keep in mind that teacher-training programs available in the t'ai chi community can range from structured, years-long curriculums to the simple approval of a teacher who tells his student one day, "Why don't you teach?" Official certificates are not necessarily the only guides. But I would suggest learning from someone who is a part of a lineage or tradition, who continues his relationship with his teacher, and who seems to be part of a larger family with t'ai chi brothers and sisters.

One area in which teachers vary is in the type of relationship they have with their students. Some teachers are very formal and their training environments are strict: students wear uniforms, observe certain rituals in training, and follow a standard curriculum. Their classes have a very definite structure; they begin and end exactly on time. The atmosphere does not encourage talking or sharing during training, and there is usually no time planned for a social tea afterward.

This formality also applies to the teacher's attitude about how the students should learn: there is only one way to learn and only one way to teach. Such a teacher can be unresponsive to the varying needs of his or her students and insists on following a certain procedure no matter what. This approach can sometimes feel so strict that we have the feeling the teacher is saying, "There is only one way. My way!"

Other teachers are more spontaneous in their presentation, and while they have a curriculum, they are ready to vary it if the situation calls for something else. Their classes have a relaxed ambiance where students can chat, drink tea, and come and go rather freely. Everyone is on a first-name basis; people go out to dinner together after training; and the instruction is at an easy, relaxed pace.

It may seem that I am painting the spontaneous teacher in more favorable terms than the formal teacher, but that is not the case. Different plants need different growing conditions. People benefit from different kinds of training approaches. The kind of soil in which we bloom may also vary from time to time and depend on where we are in our practice.

There are many instructors who teach t'ai chi exactly the way they learned it. This is not as uncreative as might be judged in modern Western pedagogic terms. These teachers believe in the way they themselves learned. It is also something that they know well; they are familiar with the stages along the way. Their expertise in helping someone else through the training process comes from their confidence and intimate knowledge of having walked the path themselves. These teachers tend to require that a student show appreciation for the tradition by faithfully following the outlined route. When a student questions the tradition or decides to train elsewhere, the teacher may feel that the student is insubordinate and violating his or her trust.

Honoring a tradition by seeking to follow it truthfully so as to discover its riches is one thing. Rote imitation and a slavish insistence on reproducing a t'ai chi form is something else. In the first instance, we are experiencing the magical process of receiving a tradition. In the second, we are drilled to repeat and mimic, to have a dead but obedient relationship to an even deader form. There is a world of difference between the two.

In receiving a t'ai chi form, there is a mutual respect not only for the tradition but for the vessel in which it is being stored. Thus any attempt by the teacher to manipulate, terrorize, dominate, or cut students down to size is incompatible not only with the t'ai chi spirit but also with basic humane interaction. There are, of course, situations where so-called tough love may be necessary, but the spirit in which such a training is carried out is always dedicated to the well-being of the student. This can be twisted, as anyone knows, and therefore it is important not to dull our good sense, especially when it comes to perceiving danger. Many of the things that have been written about selecting a spiritual teacher can also apply to choosing a t'ai chi teacher. Jack Kornfield gives a good description of the joys and pitfalls of choosing and working with a teacher in his book *A Path with Heart.*

There are other teachers who teach not only the form but also additional exercises from other movement traditions. When the introduction of such exercises into t'ai chi training is based on a solid background of practice and experience, they can be very helpful for deepening one's understanding of the form. At their best, these exercises exist in a symbiotic relationship to t'ai chi, but they are not t'ai chi. There is no substitute for the careful, gradual building of the form and the practicing of the movements over and over again.

I feel that a healthy balance of continual training in the form in all its formal aspects and the careful introduction of auxiliary exercises that have a direct and clear relationship to t'ai chi is an ideal form of training. The more advanced a t'ai chi student is, the more she can make connections between the different movement arts and experience the principles that they share.

How Do I Fit T'ai Chi into My Relationship or Family Life?

Fitting a regular practice into an intimate relationship or family life is not always easy. There are the problems of finding the time, money, and space to practice, which may be even more difficult for a person in relationship. Sometimes we have to face hostile or nonsupportive reactions from our partner or family. Or we have to hear teasing remarks or endure surprise attacks as they seek to test our skill level. Sometimes the most difficult comments are ones such as, "But I thought a t'ai chi person was not supposed to get angry . . . depressed . . . frustrated . . . excited . . . disappointed . . . smoke cigarettes," and the list goes on endlessly about how we should or should not be. The attempts to undermine us may not be very subtle at all, as when our partner or child takes the car to do nonessential shopping just before we are supposed to leave for class.

Beginning t'ai chi, which is a meditative practice, involves us in turning inward. Turning inward can be perceived as separating ourselves from others, who then feel threatened. People who are close to us may think we are not so available as before, which is partly true. Our partner, children, parents, or friends may say things like "Don't be fanatic about it!" or "Why be so extreme?" or "Do you really have to go to class tonight?" What they are really saying is, "Don't cut me off."

It's not easy to deal with the fears and projections of our

loved ones at the same time that we are trying to develop a focused practice. Different things work for different people, but if there is a bottom line, it is this: Be communicative, not missionary. People in relationship to us generally appreciate being informed, so long as they are not expected to fake some deep interest. Inviting them to visit our school or to watch us practice is a nice gesture. But be prepared to accept graciously when they decline the invitation.

Problems also appear when we are so enamored of what we are doing that we apply pressure on our loved ones to join us. Usually it's because we think it's exactly what the person needs to straighten out his or her life, deal with back pain, or whatever. And if our partnership is troubled, we believe practicing together will improve it. But our wish to help can actually be a form of arrogance. We think we have the answer, yet we don't see how unpleasant and dominating we are in trying to impose it.

Most people have to learn the hard way to ease up. At some point we see how useless it is, but there are usually a few rough spots before we do. One of the roughest is giving up the hope that we will gain a practice partner. Sometimes our loved one or friend may go so far as to attend a class or maybe take up the art. But that's rare, so stop hoping. Naturally, having a training partner is very helpful. But it doesn't have to be our partner, parent, friend, or child.

Sometimes the person we most want to reach remains hostile and nonsupporting. I won't attempt to deal with such a complex issue in just a few words. But I will say that addressing this situation involves being sensitive to others and being true to ourselves. Sometimes we are going to have to hurt the people we love. Sometimes we may have to back off from training if it becomes such an obstacle and we decide to make our relationship the priority. And sometimes we may have to split from our partner. I've seen all these variations either in my own family relationships, or in those of my students and colleagues. The bottom line for those who "succeed" in balancing their practice and relationships seems to be the degree to which the willingness to look inward as well as outward is continually renewed.

NOTES

Introduction

1. Pema Chödrön, *The Wisdom of No Escape: and the Path of Loving-kindness* (Boston: Shambhala Publications, 1991), p. 4.

Chapter 1

1. John Tarrant, *The Light Inside the Dark: Zen, Soul, and the Spiritual Life* (New York: HarperCollins, 1998), p. 185.

Chapter 6

1. Christina Feldman, *The Quest of the Warrior Woman: Women As Mystics, Healers and Guides* (San Francisco: HarperCollins, Aquarian, 1994), p. 29.

Chapter 8

1. William C. C. Chen, *Body Mechanics of T'ai Chi Chuan* (New York: William C. C. Chen, 1993), p. xxix.

Push—Exercises

1. Sharon Salzberg, *Lovingkindness: The Revolutionary Art of Happiness* (Boston: Shambhala, 1995), pp. 87–88.

Chapter 21

1. Donald D. Davis and Lawrence L. Mann, "Conservator of the Taiji Classics: An Interview with Benjamin Pang Jeng Lo," *The Journal of Asian Martial Arts 5* (1996), 4:60.

2. M. Scott Peck, *The Road Less Traveled: A New Psychology of Love, Traditional Values and Spiritual Growth* (New York: Simon and Schuster, 1978), p. 164.

Exercises—Get the Needle at the Sea Bottom

1. This exercise is based on one developed by Master Peter Ralston, parts of which were taught to me by Carol Mancuso.
2. Benjamin Pang Jeng Lo et al. *The Essence of T'ai Chi Chuan: The Literary Tradition* (Richmond: North Atlantic, 1979), p. 21.

Chapter 23

1. Mark Salzman, *Iron and Silk: Encounters with Martial Artists, Bureaucrats and Other Citizens of Contemporary China* (London: Methuen, 1986), pp. 90–91.

Chapter 24

1. Chögyam Trungpa, *Shambhala: The Sacred Path of the Warrior*, Carolyn Rose Gimian, ed. (Boulder: Shambhala, 1984), p. 46.

Chapter 25

1. Ts'ai-ken t'an, quoted in Jalaja Bonheim, *The Serpent and the Wave: A Guide to Movement Meditation* (Berkeley: Celestial Arts, 1992), p. 41.
2. Dennis Genpo Merzel, *The Eye Never Sleeps: Striking to the Heart of Zen*, Stephen Muho Proskauer, ed. (Boston: Shambhala, 1991), p. 101.

Chapter 31

1. Chödron, p. 96.

Chapter 32

1. Bonheim, p. 30.

Appendix

1. Cheng Man-ch'ing, quoted in Wolfe Lowenthal, *There Are No Secrets: Professor Cheng Man-ch'ing and His T'ai Chi Chuan* (Berkeley: North Atlantic, 1991), p. 48.

ABOUT THE AUTHOR

Linda Myoki Lehrhaupt, Ph.D., has been teaching t'ai chi and chi kung since 1982. Along with the workshops and classes she has taught over the years, she has directed three teacher-training programs where the emphasis is on t'ai chi as a meditative bodywork and its relation to health and personal development. She is also the director of one of Europe's first chi kung teacher-training programs for women. She is particularly known for her work on teaching and learning with mindfulness, and has been a teacher of mindfulness-based stress reduction since 1993.

Dr. Lehrhaupt is a Zen priest and dharma holder of Dennis Genpo Merzel, Roshi, the founder of Kanzeon Sangha. Together with her husband, artist and garden architect Norbert Wehner, she has established La Martinie, a retreat center in the Dordogne, in southwest France. Retreats in Zen meditation and meditative arts as well as t'ai chi and chi kung take place there regularly.

Contact Information
Linda Myoki Lehrhaupt can be reached at the following addresses:

Web site: *www.lehrhaupt.com*
E-mail: *LindaMyoki@hotmail.com*